Old Alston

Peter Wilkinson

Workmen, with 'trammer' (left) and carter, on the Alston Lime Co. site at the head of North Loaning c.1920. Crushed limestone, carried by narrow gauge tramway, was originally worked from Coatleyhill quarry (seen disused behind) and later from Newshield quarry beyond. Burnt in kilns (out of view left), using 'crow' coal from adjacent mines, the lime produced was carried down a steep two-foot gauge self-acting (gravity) incline to the main line (NER). Opened by Messrs Jackson, Pattinson & Lathern in 1875, these works (later nicknamed 'Linger & Die') were operated by Wm. Benson & Sons between c.1881 and 1931 and (the Revd) Walton's Alston Lime & Coal Co. from 1937 to c.1956.

© Peter Wilkinson 2009
First published in the United Kingdom, 2009,
by Stenlake Publishing Ltd.
01290 551122
www.stenlake.co.uk

ISBN 978 1 84033 463 0

The publishers regret that they cannot supply copies of any pictures featured in this book

FOREWORD

Most of the material selected for this book relates directly to the town of Alston, the most important settlement on Alston Moor and originally a major service centre for the lead industry of the North Pennine orefield. The research has examined the structure and composition of the town, looking at its streets, houses, shops and community buildings. While including much historical background information, most of the detail covers the 100 year period 1830–1930. More recent data has been included if relevant and when available. Although a location, date and brief description are always given, and some text relates only to the accompanying photograph, in other cases it is expanded to include matters not connected to the image shown. Details are sometimes provided of features which can be seen in much enlarged scanned digital images, but are not obvious at lower magnifications. Where no reliable dates are available for photos, approximations are given based on factors such as dress style, street scenery and business ownership. Generally the text is presented in a shortened form to give as much information possible in the limited space available.

Because of the geographical position and past isolation of Alston Moor, there has long been much interaction between resident families, many of whom are related. This has resulted in a fascinating but complicated social jigsaw. Whilst efforts have been made to verify information given by individuals and families and check where possible against available records, some details are conjectural and mistakes are bound to occur, considering the fallibility of both human memory and historical documents.

The many old buildings and narrow lanes give the town an ancient and picturesque appearance. Although several larger blocks of properties have been demolished, a surprising amount survives intact. Establishing accurate dates for the removal of some premises has proved problematic. Apart from postwar developments the town lacks 'official' street names. Whilst some titles have remained constant, others have changed with the passing generations or faded into obscurity. Few name plates have ever appeared.

Some businesses listed in the trade directories and gazetteers under a husband's name, who is elsewhere recorded with a different full-time occupation, were operated by the spouse or other family members, inns being a notable exception (mainly evening and weekend work). Many early dates ascribed to properties, particularly those between 1611 and 1621, actually refer to the original 999-year ground leases granted by Lord of the Manor, Henry Hilton ('Henry the Melancholy'), and not to the individual buildings. Such leases, generating only a small income by way of 'Lord's Rents' and '20 Penny Fines', but causing many complications in land and property transactions, remained in operation until recent times.

Some of the photographs and illustrations used are believed to be unique, whilst others appear in a variety of formats and are available from separate sources/collections. Copy images may be held by several different people and a number were reproduced in commercial postcard form. As well as a selection of interesting photos, some dating back to 1868, with many copied from original prints or glass plates, the book incorporates much useful historical detail regarding Alston town, its past businesses and notable residents. Several Alstonians who became celebrated outside the district are included and there is a separate section on early Alston photographers and their work.

The illustrations are roughly sequenced in the form of a downhill walk. The route (with deviations), starts from Fairhill and Townhead and descends Front Street, through the upper and lower market places to Townfoot, the station and Tyne Bridge.

AUTHOR'S COMMENTS

While every effort has been made to ensure accuracy, in a work of this kind errors are likely to occur. All are the author's responsibility for which he apologises in advance. The author would appreciate readers comments, corrections and additional information. As part of ongoing research he would also welcome details of old photographs, postcards, family records and ephemera relating to Alston Moor. Email wilkmining@tiscali.co.uk or telephone 01388 526047.

INTRODUCTION

Historical background

Alston Moor lies within the North Pennines Area of Outstanding Natural Beauty, now a UNESCO European and Global Geopark, sometimes described as England's 'last wilderness'. A protected landscape of high moorland and broad dales, with scattered settlements, it supports a surprisingly rich and diverse flora and fauna, and contains abundant remains of past industrial activity.

At the heart of the region is Alston Moor, a self-contained geographical unit bordered by some of the highest fells of the Pennine chain, from which flow the three major north-eastern rivers: the South Tyne, Tees and Wear. It is a unique area with a fascinating but anomalous history. The parish covers an area of 36,971 acres (c.58 square miles), and forms an irregular shape whose maximum size is 9½ miles both north to south and east to west. The highest point is c.2,710 feet adjoining Cross Fell summit (2,930 feet) and the lowest is Gilderdale Burn foot (787 feet). The district is drained to the north by the River South Tyne and its main tributary the River Nent.

An isolated area of heather-covered fells and lower valley meadows, Alston Moor forms a projecting part of Cumberland (Cumbria since 1974), lying to the east of the high escarpment. It adjoins Northumberland to the north (to which it is more naturally attached); Durham to the east; and (pre-1974) Westmorland to the south. Geographically, historically and commercially, the district has been more closely linked to the east of the country than the west.

Ecclesiastically, Alston has always been attached to Northumberland, being the most southerly parish of the Deanery of Corbridge and previously forming part of the Diocese of Durham. In 1882 it became part of the newly formed Diocese of Newcastle, where it still remains. Since 1987 six upper South Tyne Valley churches have comprised a 'Team Parish'.

The important Manor of Alston, incorporating the long-forgotten Manor of Garrigill, covered an area of nearly 29,000 acres (about 45 square miles). It was smaller than the parish as it excluded 'Priorsdale', a large tract of land transferred in c.1215 to the Priory of Hexham by the de Veteripont family. After dissolution in about 1536, Priorsdale (Presdale) fell into private hands, being divided in 1588 into three separate 'Liberties' – Eshgill, Hole and Hill. The Manor was later very valuable, the Lords (Greenwich Hospital) reporting in 1821 that the mines yielded annual produce of £100,000 and the lands about £1,200.

The early history of the area is rather obscure, with little evidence to date of prehistoric occupation, other that

a few stray finds and two small Bronze Age burial mounds at Kirkhaugh. Some of the early place names indicate a sparse resident Celtic population, but it was the Romans who left the more striking legacy of their occupation. The little known Whitley Castle fort, lying about two miles north-west of Alston, was occupied from the mid-second to the end of the fourth century. Unspoilt and with an almost unique complex of defensive ramparts, the commanding site is on the Maiden Way Roman road, which runs from Greenhead to Kirby Thore. The extent of a wider Roman influence in the district and possible involvement in lead mining has yet to be established.

The Dark Ages saw an influx of Anglo-Saxon invaders and settlers, followed by Danes/Norwegians (Vikings), who again left their mark in place names. The period approaching and following the Norman Conquest becomes confusing, although documentary evidence begins to appear at this stage. Alston Moor became part of the Franchise of Tynedale (or 'Tindale'), an area stretching north to the Scottish border. It formed an English estate held by the King of Scotland, but with the mineral rights retained by the English Crown. By c.1160, and long after, the district was administered on behalf of the Scottish Crown by the Norman de Veteriponte family who were the first Lords of the Manor of Alston. With the mining community independently controlled and protected by the English king, there was much unrest and many grievances, particularly as the mines were very valuable during the twelfth and thirteenth centuries. Lead was in great demand for building work and the high silver content was used for coinage (supplied to the royal mint at Carlisle). At this time the area was permanently confirmed as part of Cumberland.

By the early 1400s, both manor and mines (which had greatly reduced in value) were controlled by the Stapleton family, who were related through marriage to the de Veteripontes. In 1469 the estate passed, again by marriage, to the Hiltons of Hilton Castle (Sunderland), in whose hands the manor remained for 160 years. It was Henry Hilton who, in 1611, began leasing out much copyhold land (but excluding the mineral rights) on 999 year leases to raise money for his daughter's marriage dowry. In 1629 he sold the manor outright, including the mines, 'said to be nearly exhausted', to Sir Edward Radcliffe for £2,500.

It remained in Radcliffe hands until 1715 when it was forfeited to the Crown after James, the 3rd Earl of Derwentwater, took part in the first Jacobite Rebellion, for which he was beheaded in February 1716. In 1734/35, all the Derwentwater Estates, including Alston Moor, were passed to the Royal Greenwich Hospital for Seamen as a source of revenue for the upkeep of that establishment. Under this unusual arrangement the area was administered from London by the Admiralty (and Treasury), under whose control the mineral wealth was carefully exploited, much to the benefit of the steadily expanding population. In 1964, after 229 years of Greenwich Hospital management, the Alston estates were transferred in their entirety to a body with similar objectives, the Trustees for Roman Catholic Purposes.

The modern term 'geodiversity' epitomises the unique relationship within this district between geology, landscape and human activity. A founding place for the study of stratigraphy, as well as the subject of seminal works and home to pioneering geologists, Alston Moor became one of the richest lead mining areas in the British Isles. It forms part of the structural geological unit known as the 'Alston Block', an uplifted region bounded by three large faults, the sedimentary Carboniferous Limestone Series rocks gently dipping to the east. Near-vertical fractures in the alternating layers of limestones, sandstones, shales and narrow coal seams were later infilled with hot mineral solutions which formed ore-bearing veins. These contain a wide variety of commercially important minerals such as lead (with silver), zinc, copper, fluorspar and baryte, which have all been mined on Alston Moor, along with iron ore and coal.

With little current evidence of mining in the Roman era, and none for the Dark Ages, the documentary history of lead/silver mining begins in 1130 (Pipe Rolls, Henry I) and continues through the important twelfth and thirteenth century period, with references to the 'Silver Mine of Carlisle' (identified with Alston) and the royal Carlisle mint. Although the mines later became less significant, Crown interest and control continued into the sixteenth century and possibly beyond ('Mines Royal') because of the silver content of the lead.

The second half of the seventeenth century saw the appearance of many small companies working vein leases let by the Radcliffe family. It was only after 1735, however, under Greenwich Hospital management, that the industry really began to develop and rapidly expand, being strictly controlled through a hierarchical system directed locally by two Receivers, a Moormaster and Bailiff. Whilst numerous small concerns existed, the largest to emerge after 1745 was the London Lead Co. which continued to grow and became the most powerful and influential organisation in this and adjoining districts. Originally a Quaker concern, it was a well organised, benevolent and philanthropic company, displaying a strong social conscience. Supporting hundreds of families, it was heavily involved in many aspects of life on Alston Moor, including education, religion and social welfare. It is perhaps best known for its vast lead mining and smelting complex at Nenthead, where it built a new 'model-village' between c.1822–28.

The economic expansion of the first half of the nineteenth century gave way to a gradual downturn, followed after 1870 by a rapid decline. Less productive ground, rising costs, falling lead prices and cheap imported ores had a devastating effect on the industry, and in 1882 the London Lead Co. left the district. It was succeeded by the Nenthead & Tynedale Lead & Zinc Company which struggled on until 1895. With mining in a near terminal state, a rapidly shrinking population and the local economy turning to agriculture, the Vieille Montagne Zinc Co. of Liege, Belgium took over. An international corporation, it reopened the Nenthead and other mines for zinc, introduced new technology, and with a large capital investment and development programme

THE COBBLER'S EPITAPH

My cutting board's to pieces split,
My size-sticks will no measures mete,
My rotten last's turned into holes,
My blunted knife cuts no more soles,
My hammer's head' flown from the haft,
No more Saint Mondays with the craft,
My nippers, pincers, stirrup and rag
And all my kit have got the bag;
My lapstone's broke, my colour's o'er,
My gum-glass froze, my paste's no more;
My heels sewed on, my pegs are driven,
I hope I'm on the road to heaven.

FROM A TOMBSTONE IN ALSTON CHURCHYARD, CUMBRIA

brought a renewed vigour to the area. VMZ Co. extraction ceased at Nenthead in 1920, but continued sporadically elsewhere until final closure in 1947.

Quarrying, an industry still active today, has always been important, with most of the properties and their slated roofs – along with endless miles of fell and field walls – being constructed of local sandstone. Limestone was used for road-making, rail ballast and lime production, whilst coal mining has only recently ceased after several centuries. The extraction of copper, iron ore, fluorspar, baryte, witherite, umber and ochre has also taken place in the district.

Agriculture and mining have always been closely linked on Alston Moor, although the two activities were not compatible under the civil framework existing at an earlier period. In the dual system which evolved during the twelfth century, the lead (and silver) miners lived in independent communities ('shiels') under royal protection. Being self-governing with the power to elect their own Coroner and King's Sergeant to administer law and order – and therefore outside manorial authority – many disputes arose. During the fifteenth century, these rights were extinguished as control of the mines and manor merged under the Stapleton family.

Farming in this isolated region evolved from a system of 'shieldings' (shields, sheals, etc.), or sites where livestock were grazed on higher ground with adjoining temporary dwellings. Initially established along the more fertile valley bottoms and lower slopes, they developed into permanent settlements. At least 68 shieldings are recorded in 1315 in the Manor of Alston Moor, then in the possession of Nicholas de Veteriponte. They formed the basis of the later farm tenements (house and land), a similar number of which, 66, were granted between 1611 and 1621 by Henry Hilton on 999 year leases (although they were later subdivided amongst increasing numbers of named tenants). The valley bottom farming area was originally contained within a boundary 'earthen wall and ditch'. This protected the hay meadows and fields from the livestock, which were driven out on to the unenclosed fells during the summer months of May to August. Strict rules relating to both animal movements and civil control were contained in two Alston Moor codes of law, first drawn up in the reign of Henry VII (1485–1509) and revised in 1597 (the 39th year of Elizabeth I's reign).

The Paine Roll (dated 1597, copied 1692) lists 50 fines imposed for mainly civil offences by the Manor Court, later held at Lowbyer. Some regulations were local, whilst others incorporated statutory law, with a number applied to farming matters, including dates when tenants should go to the 'sheals'. The Drift [Drive] Roll (1597, copied 1683) describes the designated routes for c.52 farm tenements, for driving their livestock on to the open 'ffells'. Both documents suggest summer shields in some form continued into the seventeenth century.

The later demand for miner/farmer smallholdings, which left an indelible stamp on the landscape, saw much fell land improved and enclosed. Farms up to heights of 1,500 feet – and in exceptional cases 1,800 feet – were won from the 'wastes' by drainage and extensive use of lime and manure. Strongly promoted by the London Lead Co., the system improved health, encouraged worker stability and provided basic food supplies. After the collapse of mining, agriculture gradually became the mainstay of the district.

By the late eighteenth century, lead mining had become the principal economic support for Alston Moor. As the industry flourished and the population expanded (peaking in 1831 and 1851), a wealth of services developed, often supported by the London Lead Co. and Greenwich Hospital. The market town of Alston became the main service and distribution centre for the region.

Originally linked by a network of packhorse ('galloway') routes over the wild and desolate fells, and later by a few rough, stony roads, the first turnpike 'upgrade' came in 1778, followed by another in 1793/94. However, it was not until an 1824 Act of Parliament and the engineering of a new complex of Alston Turnpike Trust roads by the famous J.L. MacAdam, that good communications were

Now demolished part of Grisdale's Lane, looking towards Front Street (c.1900/1910)

finally established. Construction began in 1824 and had been completed by 1830. The first coach ('The Balloon') commenced running between Hexham, Alston and Penrith in September 1828.

Increasing prosperity led to the opening of the 13-mile Alston to Haltwhistle branch railway in 1852, which greatly improved links with the outside world. The line finally closed in 1976, after several reprieves due to Alston's remoteness and the lack of a reliable alternative winter route.

Improvements in administration, civil amenities and public health continued throughout the nineteenth century. A fresh water supply was piped into the town in 1808 with stand pipe taps erected later, the same utility being installed at Nenthead in 1848/50 by the London Lead Co. This company also introduced medical services with a resident doctor/surgeon serving the district as early as the 1820s, and there was a continual improvement in sanitary conditions (including public wash house and baths, 1867). Consequently, the epidemics which regularly blighted other communities were rare on Alston Moor. The Board of Guardians took on the role of Rural Sanitary Authority in 1872 and the Rural District Council was established in December 1894.

The Alston Gas Light & Coke Co. first supplied gas to the town in 1843 and continued in production until 1960. The electricity power line into the area (over Hartside fell) was not installed until 1934. In 1850 the police station with its courtroom, cells and officer's dwelling was completed, and a grand neo-Gothic town hall with attached Savings Bank (est. 1825) opened in 1858.

Religion, especially Methodism, had an enormous impact on the district during the nineteenth century. The

WILLIAM DAVIES STEPHENS (1827-1901)

William Davies Stephens is now unknown in Alston, despite being one of the town's most distinguished sons and an 'illustrious citizen of Newcastle', where a large monument was erected in his memory.

He was born at Lowbyer, Alston, in 1827, where his father James (from Cornwall) was a Greenwich Hospital agent for nearly 40 years. Having been educated at the Grammar School, he worked at the Tyneside chemical works of another Alstonian, the famous Hugh Lee Pattinson, for thirteen years. In 1864 the shipping company Stephens set up with William Laing merged to form the new 'Tyne Steam Shipping Co. Ltd.' of which he was later managing director, then chairman. This developed into a large and flourishing concern operating between the Tyne, London and major continental ports. Amongst its eminent board members were James Leathart (b.1820, Alston, managing partner of Locke, Blackett & Co. lead works, Newcastle) and secretary (later managing director) Richard Welford, a noted Tyneside historian, literary and commercial figure and property owner at Alston.

In 1873, Stephens, by then well established in business, entered upon 'a long and eminently useful career' in public life. He was elected a city councillor and a governor of the Royal Victoria Infirmary in 1874, Sheriff of Newcastle in 1879, JP and Lord Mayor in 1887/88 and Alderman in 1890. In addition, he was a Wesleyan Methodist trustee, as well as a committee member and officer of the Ragged School, Sailors' Society, Sick Children's Hospital ('The Fleming'), YMCA, Northern Counties Orphanage and many more philanthropic bodies.

A major temperance reformer, Stephens was known as the 'Gospel Temperance bishop', 'his power recognised all over the kingdom'. In this capacity, he was 'head-centre' of a group of 46,000 pledge members who helped close 139 public houses and three breweries. In 1882 his efforts resulted in the establishment of the great summer Temperance Festival, held annually during Race Week in June to counter the 'saturnalia' of the Miner's Derby etc. This took place on the city's Town Moor and was the forerunner of the current 'Hoppings', reputedly the world's largest non-permanent (and still temperate!) fair.

Always retaining close links with Alston (house at The Highlands), Alderman 'Danny' Stephens was described as 'one of the busiest men in a busy city with remarkable vitality, genial disposition, tact and energy'. He died aged 74 on 8 December 1901 after a lingering illness.

church at Alston was founded in the twelfth century, and the Chapelry of Garrigill (Gerard's Gill) was attached to it by 1215. The parish formed part of the Diocese of Durham until 1882, when it was transferred to Newcastle. St Augustine's Church at Alston was rebuilt in 1770 and again in 1869/70. A new vicarage was erected in 1812 by its ever-supportive patrons, the Greenwich Hospital, and another added at Garrigill in 1851 to house a permanent curate. Nenthead became a separate parish in 1845, when St John's Church was built, with a vicarage provided by the London Lead Co.

Nonconformism, which later engulfed the district, first emerged at Garrigill where a group of 'Dissenters' put up a small cottage chapel between 1690 and 1700 at Loaning Head. They erected a larger Congregational (Independent) Chapel at nearby Redwing in 1756, adding another at Alston (Gossipgate) in 1804, which operated until c.1977.

While the upper/wealthier classes often remained within the Anglican church, it was Methodism which evolved and dominated local society. Divisions among Alston's Wesleyans in the early 1820s saw large numbers – particularly miners and some radicals – join the new Primitive Methodist movement. For both groups, Alston was an 'exceptional' area, presenting a unique challenge in isolated and harsh surroundings, with the miners and small farmers noted for their intelligence, fervour and independent spirit.

After being 'missioned' in the 1740s and visited by John Wesley in 1748, what was reputed to be the first chapel in Cumberland was erected at Townfoot, Alston, in 1760. A replacement was built at Overburn in 1797, and was followed by St Paul's at Townhead in 1868, a large and conspicuous structure representing the peak of Wesleyan influence. An extensive hall/schoolroom was added as late as 1933. Other early chapels followed at Tynehead (by 1788?), Garrigill c.1790 (they had used the old 'Dissenters'

chapel from c.1765) and Nenthead c.1775. Throughout the following century numerous additional and replacement buildings were erected. Having been previously attached to the Hexham area, Alston formed its own circuit in 1808.

Differences among the Wesleyans in the 1820s – more to do with practice than belief – saw the district rapidly adopt Primitive Methodism, becoming a 'hotbed' of the movement and the most famous circuit in Cumberland. Primitive Methodism appealed to the poorer working classes who were attracted to 'a more exciting, cheaper and less status-conscious religion'. They became known as 'Ranters' after critics described their sometimes noisy and enthusiastic activities as the 'ravings of religious fanatics'. In 1823, Nenthead and Garrigill were 'missioned' by preachers from Westgate (Weardale), and Alston by those from Hexham, with new chapels erected in all three places in 1825. Nentsberry (1829) and several others followed, most later being rebuilt and enlarged. Alston Moor formed its own circuit in 1835/6 and remained a Primitive Methodist stronghold with regular huge revivals which 'set the villages on fire'.

Both Methodist groups organised rallies, excursions, picnics and 'demonstrations' of faith. They fervently supported the temperance movement and youth organisations such as the Band of Hope, and by about 1840 most chapels incorporated Sunday Schools. However, the collapse of the mining industry, large-scale migration and later the effects of the First World War resulted in dwindling congregations. The two branches of Methodism united in 1932, with subsequent chapel closures.

By contrast, the Society of Friends never really flourished, despite the early (pre-1750) Quaker roots of the London Lead Co., which had such a long-term benevolent influence on the district. The current Alston Meeting House, built in 1732, has supported only small congregations, while that

Invoice, 1826, John Litell, blacksmith

at Wellgill, Nenthead (dated 1724) had closed within 50 years. Excluding numerous *in situ* reconstructions, at least 28 places of worship existed within the parish during the eighteenth and nineteenth centuries.

The other great influence in the district was education, which was closely linked to the expansion of the lead industry, increased economic growth and the rapid spread of religion. A great educative upsurge took place during the first half of the nineteenth century, promoted and financially assisted by the London Lead Co. and Greenwich Hospital, with pupil numbers rising from *c.*210 (boys only) in 1805 to about 1,000 in 1822. Schools had been established at an early period, with Alston Grammar, which was rebuilt in 1828, possibly dating from the late sixteenth century. Garrigill Parochial School (rebuilt 1811) dated from about 1685. Tynehead (Dorthgill) School, said to exist in 1788, was rebuilt at Leehouse Well as a combined school and Wesleyan chapel in 1822. A similar dual-purpose building at Foulard, Nenthead, dating to 1774 and later relocated to the village centre, was supported by the London Lead Co. A plan of 1773 shows an 'old School House' (possibly *c.*1766) near Dowgang Mine, Nenthead, while others were erected by public subscription at both Leadgate (*c.*1775) and Nenthall (1789).

A radical new phase of education began at Nenthead in 1819 with the opening of the first London Lead Co. school. This was nondenominational and catered for both boys and girls. The system initiated at the school, which later helped set the national standard, required compulsory pupil attendance up to the age of twelve (as well as at chapel/ church and Sunday School!) for future employment with the company, which generously supported educational development over a wide area. A workmen's reading/news room and library followed in 1833 (rebuilt *c.*1859), and a large new school was erected in 1864. This was replaced in 1899 by a state Board School. Other local mining companies also supported education – Nenthall School was rebuilt by the Hudgill Burn Co. in 1848 and Leadgate by the Rotherhope Fell Co. in 1850. By 1842 there were seven libraries in the area, four in the town of Alston.

The 'British' and 'National' societies (later government-aided) were amongst the charitable religious bodies which established schools within the district. At Alston, the National School (mixed) was built at Townhead in 1811, with a subscription library added in 1821. Variously known as the Charity, Free and High School, and latterly the 'Topp', it was rebuilt in 1884 and became a Public Elementary in 1909. The National Church of England School for Girls was erected in 1844 and the adjoining infants' school in 1851. They were subsequently known as the 'Salvin Schools' after the vicar and principal benefactor, Revd Hugh Salvin. The provisions of the 1902 Balfour Education Act (which saw closure of Alston School Board – formed in 1892), were finally implemented in 1909 with the construction of Samuel King's Secondary School and reorganisation of the High School.

The Parochial School in Garrigill village centre was supplemented by a Girls' British School, erected in 1851 at Gatefoot alongside the new library (built in 1848). A boys' school was attached in 1872, the two amalgamating in 1874 to become the 'United Schools'.

Continued enlightenment was encouraged and catered for by the many libraries, reading/news rooms, a Literary & Philosophical Society and several Mechanics' Institutes. Excluding a Ladies College, Dame and other private schools, at least eighteen educational establishments existed on Alston Moor up to the early twentieth century.

Alston town

Alston lies in a remote location at the meeting point of five main routes (four over high passes), with two important bridged river crossings. At least sixteen spellings of the town's name have been recorded in the past, including Austen, Aldstone and Aldeston. Reputedly the highest market town in England, with weekly markets on a Saturday, it held six fairs a year in the later nineteenth century.

Traditionally Alston has been a stopping place for travellers on longer journeys. By road it is 19 miles to Penrith, 29 to Carlisle, 24 to Hexham and 45 to Newcastle. The original rail link to Haltwhistle was 13 miles long. The town is situated near the confluence of the rivers Nent and South Tyne, on the east bank of the latter at the north-west foot of Middle Fell. It lies on a steep hillside, with the railway station located at the lowest point (865 feet). Ascending the main street, Townfoot is at 921 feet, the Market Place 968 feet and Townhead at 1,043 feet.

To date, little is known of early or medieval Alston. One of its first descriptions – by William Hutchinson, who visited during a storm in 1776 – paints a gloomy picture:

'It is a small market town, meanly built, situated on the declivity [downward slope] of a steep hill, inhabited by miners … in a mountainous, barren and inhospitable country. Pent in a narrow valley … the wind tempestuous … impending clouds … rain beating vehemently against the windows [of the inn] … Two fair days together … were seldom known in this country'.

JOSEPH HALL, CLOCKMAKER

Joseph Hall (b.1767), outstanding Alston and Cumberland clockmaker and later owner of Low Mill (1814–25), married Elizabeth Bustin at Stanhope in 1794. Having moved to Alston he built at least five known clocks, two of which are of exceptional quality. One of these was for the couple's new home (the converted first Wesleyan chapel) and featured two superimposed finely engraved silvered dials. It was inscribed 'Joseph & Elizabeth Hall, Alston 1797'. He removed the chimes in 1804 when he became a Quaker. The other was made for his parents-in-law and featured a brass arched dial. It was inscribed 'Made for Anthony & Elizabeth Bustin by Joseph Hall, Alston 1800'. He moved to Wigton in 1825, dying at Waverton in 1843, aged 76.

Unfortunately, his views were perpetuated for over a century, with the word 'mean' (i.e. poor, cheap or shabby) being repeatedly used. Snippets from successive – but often diverse – accounts add to a broader image. 'Universal' (c.1791) found the area 'romantic and pleasant … but, by reason of the lead mines [it] is uncommonly populous'. 'Jollies' (1811) stated, 'The town of Aldston … is almost wholly inhabited by miners, or people connected with that employ', but the buildings 'are rather mean and disagreeable'. Thomas Sopwith (1833) noted, 'It contains about 400 houses and is on the whole rather meanly built. The streets are inconveniently steep and narrow'. He added that the weekly markets were unusually busy. Historian Revd J. Hodgson (1840) was more impressed: 'It hangs on a green hillside, fronting the west, and consists of two main streets [he includes the Hexham to Penrith turnpike road through Townfoot] … Its white and slated houses are all of stone … and look gay and cheerful'. Rebutting Hutchinson's climate comment, he noted that 'in 1825 it enjoyed 250 fair-weather days'.

Visiting Alston in its heyday, London writer/wayfarer Walter White (1859) recognised the beauty of the surrounding 'wide rolling expanses', but found the town 'hilly, irregular, and shabby', which was what he expected of an 'isolated metropolis of the mining region'. He wrote: 'The principal street is so steep that you will pant again on the way through the [two] market places to the upper part of the town … stop and look at the hard-featured houses and the curious shops, among which there is a good display of mining gear and implements … not a poor town, it has £20,000 in the Savings Bank … pays some attention to drainage and water supply … and is a good centre for excursions.'

Later described as 'the most eastern town in the county [Cumberland]', author and travelling salesman J.W. Allen (1878) saw it as Mr Pickwick (Charles Dickens) did Bath: 'It is very much like the perpendicular street a man sees in a dream, and which he cannot get up for the life of him'. In his long description he notes: 'the houses appear to have been stuck down anywhere … respectable shops, a brewery, a large cloth factory … several inns [16], and two very good hotels … well supplied with water … gas in the streets and houses … good library'. He thought Alston 'grossly libelled' by a recent Hutchinson-type portrayal, adding 'It is vastly different now to what it was at the close of the last century', much more accessible with a 'cheerful and civilized appearance'.

Fifty years later and with mining having given way to agriculture, perceptions had changed. What in the nineteenth century was old, rather plain and lacking in 'architectural ornaments' was by the 1930s being seen as quaint, historic and picturesque. 'Mean' became the new 'romantic'. There was consensus amongst writers of every era, however, that the town was unplanned, with many of its buildings 'irregularly placed'.

Edmund Vale ('North Country', 1937) wrote, 'I do not think there is a more mediaeval-looking town in the whole county'. Remarking on its lack of 'ordinary' streets other than the 'one thoroughfare leading downhill through two separate [market] squares', he was intrigued by the

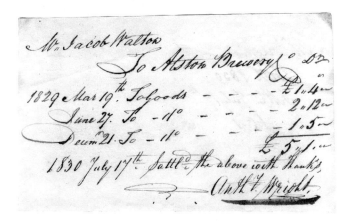

Brewery invoice to Jacob Walton, Greenends, 1829

assemblage of narrow cobbled lanes and alleys, outside stairs and courtyards 'stuffed with strange buildings'. He thought 'the beauty and quaintness of the place' should be preserved.

The famous Arthur Wainwright, who visited in 1938, was similarly impressed: 'It is the only town which really lies in the heart of the Pennines … I saw Alston for the first time, falling away from me in a chaotic jumble of rooftops down to the green valley below. The town clings to a hillside so steep that the houses seem to be piled one on top of another; and an odd assortment they are, of many shapes and sizes, all old, all built of stone'. His final evocative words perhaps epitomise the last phase of 'Old Alston' in those halcyon days before the impending doom of the second war:

'But Alston is not seen by parading the main street, old and picturesque though this is. The straggling rows of buildings that flank the street are a mask to the real face of the town. Turn along one of the narrow alleys, follow its twisting course until you are lost in a maze of branching lanes, in a confusion of tottering buildings, set most oddly and bewilderingly at all angles. This is Alston and, when you have delved deep into it, the main thoroughfare becomes, by comparison, a Regent Street.'

Inhabitants

Early writers were more complimentary about the inhabitants of Alston than the town itself. This trend continued, with later accounts describing the population in exemplary terms with regards to education, religion and moral character. Descriptions up to the early twentieth century concentrate predominantly on the mining community. While many male workers, both in town and country, had dual occupations, most households and families included members connected with the lead mining industry. Unfortunately there was a high mortality rate amongst underground workers, predominantly from 'dust diseases of the lungs'. A Board of Health Report (1858) records that Alston is 'the most exclusively lead mining district in England … in which there is a larger proportion of widows than any other place in the kingdom'.

William Hutchinson (1794) noted, 'Most of the men are miners … they shew a simplicity of manners, rarely found among other labouring people. Mining renders them, later in manhood, unhealthy, and the strongest seldom exceed 60 years of age' (average life expectancy was 45–50).

Most of the nineteenth century writers express similar views, the main points of which are summarised in the following two examples. E. Mackenzie (1825) wrote, 'The miners are a peculiarly hardy, active, and intelligent class of men … as much distinguished for an unbending spirit of independence as for intellectual activity and acquirements … Their moral habits in domestic life are respectable, and they are particularly distinguished for the virtues of charity and hospitality'. He added that although their work was 'extremely hazardous and uncertain', it involved a knowledge of arithmetic, machinery, geology and chemistry and they were noted for 'correctness of judgement'.

A.F. Foster, Assistant Commissioner (State of popular education in England, Royal Commission report, 1861) was particularly impressed with what he found: 'The lead miners are remarkably intelligent and generally well educated … They consist of families who have lived for ages on the spot … A steady, provident, orderly, and industrious people … high minded … disdaining pauperism … subject to very little or no mixture for ages past, as appears by their language … Attendance on public worship is the rule, not the exception, and profane language is scarcely ever heard'. He acknowledged the London Lead Co.'s superior system of education, particularly that schooling was strictly compulsory. Much of what he saw was embodied in the famous 1870 Education Act, which established a national scheme of elementary schools, with compulsory attendance by 1880.

Advert, 1882 (old Sun Inn premises)

Roadmen and carters on the Nenthead road (now A689) near Middle Skelgill, looking west towards Clitheroe and Townhead c.1920. They are using crushed whinstone or limestone to repair a section of 'macadamised' or 'metalled' road.

John Lowden MacAdam (1756–1836), eminent road-maker and surveyor, brought his new method of road construction to the district in 1824 when he began work on the network of routes under the control of the Alston Turnpike Trust. His system involved compacting and bonding three layers of small broken stone to form a 10 inch thick surface. Later, a fine 'binding' coat of chippings and dust, sprayed with water, could be rolled out to a smooth finish. The advent of motor vehicles with greater speeds, the 'sucking' action of rubber tyres and demands for dustless roads and more durable surfaces, saw the gradual introduction of 'tarmacadaming'.

Lead mining was the main stimulus for road development in the North Pennines. Until the late eighteenth century the distribution of goods relied on pack horses using rough fell tracks, which were often impassable in winter. Improved toll roads operated by turnpike trusts did not penetrate the orefield until 1778, when the Hexham to Alston route was upgraded. The Lobley Hill Turnpike opened from Gateshead to Cowshill in 1793 and by 1794 had been extended through Nenthead and Alston. In 1824 this was combined with other routes under the newly formed Alston Turnpike Trust.

The driver of the Marshall steamroller is Jack White, who later became a Newcastle Corporation driver. Bobby Hodgson (b.1879, Alston), a roadman from youth whose father was a coal miner, is standing below holding his son John's hand. To the right are carters Thomas Place (standing) and Wesley Armstrong (seated). Thomas (b.1871, Alston) was one of a long line of farmers and carters from nearby Low Skelgill. He died in 1947, aged 76. Other roadmen at the time included T. Cousin, H. Millican and A. Varty. Close by at Blagill road end was the Skelgill Toll House, long since demolished.

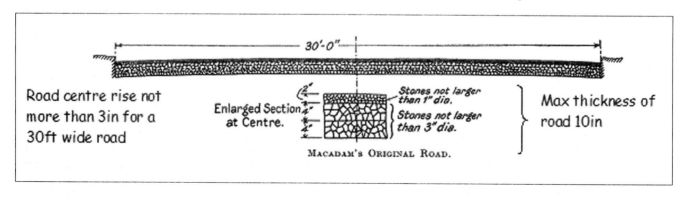

CHAPEL TERRACE, ALSTON

Few old photographs exist of the dozen or so properties in Chapel Terrace, running from Jollybeard Lane (by the tree) to the Forge at Townhead, and external views of the Primitive Methodist Chapel, left, are scarce. The houses between the chapel and lane, originally 'Snowdon's Buildings', along with other properties in the Butts and at Townfoot were owned by the Snowdon family, who operated as stonemasons and builders for over a hundred years from the 1820s. Early twentieth century developments, beyond Jollybeard Lane up the Nenthead road, began with white gabled Avondale Villa (Mary A. Parmley) attached to Kentmere House (Harrop Holmes, blacksmith). From 1910 the gap beyond was infilled up to Hillcroft, seen on the rise at Broadpot Hill. (A small German POW camp was built in the field adjoining this property at the end of WWII. It was administered from the large Merry Thought Camp at Calthwaite, near Penrith.)

Whilst the later St Augustine's Church had a strong physical presence in the town centre, the hearts and minds of many of the population during the nineteenth century were strongly influenced by nonconformist ideology, represented in the main by Methodism. There were at least 14 chapels operating in the district, the area being a centre of religious fervour, fuelled by educational advancement.

In the 1740s Alston was 'missioned' by Wesleyan Methodists, whose Townfoot chapel (built in 1760) was the first in Cumberland. By the early nineteenth century Methodism had spread throughout the country, attracting a large membership. Administration became a problem and divisions occurred within the organisation, resulting in the foundation of the Society of Primitive Methodism, often referred to as 'Ranters', in 1810.

In about 1820, unrest amongst Alston's Wesleyans saw a shift towards the new group, which offered a more exciting, cheaper and less status conscious form of religion. It put

Harvest Festival, c.1910

power and control into the hands of lay representatives, which appealed to the working classes.

After being linked to both the Hexham and Westgate (Weardale) branches, Alston formed its own circuit in 1835/6. Described as a 'hotbed of Primitivism', this was the most famous circuit in Cumberland and remained a stronghold well into the twentieth century.

The first chapel dated from 1823, although its rear lintel was inscribed 'PMC 1825'. Poorly constructed and said to be 'in danger of early collapse', it was replaced in 1845 at a cost of £300, with members providing free labour and materials. The chapel was renovated in 1888 to accommodate 130 people. Its unusual semi-octagonal extension, which contained stairs and a vestry, may have been added later. The Wesleyan and Primitive movements united in 1932 and the chapel closed in December 1940. Two years later it was converted into a school canteen (seating 104 people) and classroom by Cumberland County Council. In 1962 it was rebuilt as two houses and the projecting section demolished.

This *c.*1901 view of the Fair Hill area at Townhead is entitled 'Alston New Recreation Ground' and was taken by Hugh Walton of Alston. Originally known as Potter's Fields, it was a camping ground where potters and tinkers sold their wares. From an early period annual fairs for cattle, sheep, horses and pigs were held here, the largest taking place at the end of May. An agricultural society was formed in 1839, holding its annual show in October.

The white building on the left of the picture is the old ropery, which was operated by William Boucock from the late 1820s to the early 1880s. It was later converted into four cottages. Below the ropery is the High School and Police Station.

In the early nineteenth century the land owners and Lords of the Manor, Greenwich Hospital, built a new dam here across the Overburn to replace a smaller one downstream, behind the old grammar school. Later, as well as powering a forge, two corn mills and two sawmills, the water was used for street cleaning and sewage disposal.

In 1808, partly to avoid pollution caused by lead mining, a new 'clean' water supply was brought from springs on nearby Broadpot Hill and fed in lead pipes to four pants (public wells) within the town. The Fair Hill area was also walled, incorporating three 10-foot wide entrances with whalebone gateposts. By 1890, Alston's water supply came from one large tank at Townhead which supplied seven pillar taps.

In December 1894 the new Alston with Garrigill Rural District Council (RDC) was formed. This replaced the Rural Sanitary Board and used its additional 'Urban Powers' to deal with the ongoing problems of water supplies, waste and sewage disposal. The dumping of offal and 'night soil' in the Fair Hill area was a particular issue. Council records from the late 1890s and early 1900s describe the laying of new water and sewage mains, to which residents were obliged to apply for connection. 'Public ashpits' and a 'urinal' followed as part of this process. Despite the improvements, some waste seems to have still ended up in the Mill Race (Burn), as reported in the *Cumberland & Westmorland Herald* on 23 February 1907.

An 1898 appeal to mark Queen Victoria's Diamond Jubilee set out to raise funds for a town recreation ground. Its proposers described how 'succeeding generations of children have had no place for their games, and the bigger boys have had to find open spaces where they could play … sometimes damaging walls and grass, also causing great annoyance to occupiers and owners' [sounds familiar!]. In May 1899, the town bought the two Fair Hill fields from Greenwich Hospital to carry out this project. The purchase price of £276/7/6d was described as 'little more than half market value', although the 5.8 acre site was apparently 'bleak and bare'. Creating the recreation ground cost over £400, with the open mill race culverted at a later date. The lower ground was used as an ashtip and the annual fairs continued to use the site free of charge.

During the 1930s Depression, local labour was employed to landscape the infilled ashtip area and build a pavilion, tennis courts and bowling green. Part of the latter collapsed into the race below in 1952.

1. Account extract, *c.*1808. 2. OS map 25 inch first edition, 1859. 3. Fair Hill dam and water courses, Greenwich Hospital estate plan, *c.*1825. 4. School sewerage into Mill Burn. *Cumberland & Westmorland Herald*, 23 February 1907

1

CASH PAID TO SUNDRIES FOR BRINGING
THE WATER
INTO ALSTON.

	£.	s.	d.
Cutting and Covering the Conduit from the Fountain Head to the Reservoir; Cutting the Ground and Covering the Pipes from the Reservoir to the Potatoe-Market, Cross, and to the Vicarage Wall, as per Acct. delivered	84	19	2
Mr Lowry for Lead - - - - - - -	39	0	0
Ralph Longstaff for casting & laying Pipes	25	0	0
Thomas Craig for Paving - - - - -	2	17	6
Messrs. Snowden and Mowberry Mason Work	19	12	0
Edmund Bulman, for Smith Work - - -	6	8	3
John Harrop, Ale for Workmen - - - -	6	18	0
Coals for the Plumbers - - - - - -	3	2	10
Joseph Watson, for leading Clay, &c. - -	5	10	3
John Lee, Mason Work - - - - - -	0	8	0
Jonathan Walton for removing Rubbish - -	0	8	0
Walter Litell for Damage done - - - -	1	1	0
John Little for Flag Stones - - - - -	1	1	0
Thomas Atkinson for Work done - - - -	1	13	2
Joseph Walton, for Work done - - - -	1	8	0
John Walton for Work done - - - - -	0	4	6
John Bell for Carpenter's Work - - - -	0	11	0
Cord for Plumbers - - - - - - -	0	1	0
Elizabeth Carr for Fog - - - - - -	0	1	0
T. Walton & Co. for Printing - - - -	0	12	0
	£200	16	8

3

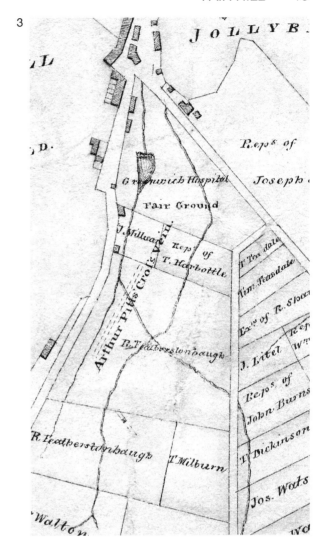

2

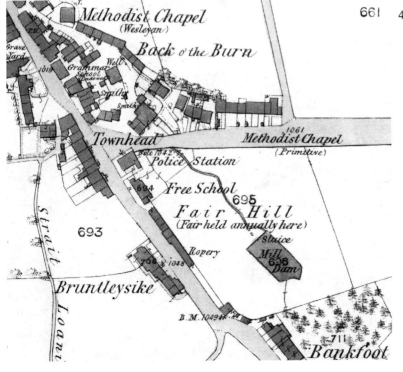

661

4

ALSTON HIGH SCHOOL.

A letter was received from the managers of the above school asking permission to connect their closets with the Fair Hill water course, commonly known as The Burn.

The Sanitary Inspector and the Clerk thought that the Council should be very careful in granting such a request, for there had been a similar application that day.

The Clerk: Isn't this water used by two millers?

Mr J. R. Walton: If we object where can it go to?

Mr. Bramwell explained that an estimated sum of £250 was being spent on improvements by raising the playground altering the closets, etc., at this school, and it would mean a considerably increased outlay if this request were not granted. The sewer that the District Council had made emptied itself into the burn, and he could see no reason why the school sewerage should not be emptied directly into the Burn instead of it being taken (at additional expense which would have to be paid for largely by the local ratepayers) into the sewer and ultimately into the Burn.

Looking east up 'Ranter Bank' from Townhead, c.1896. Alston's police station (right) was built on the ancient pinfold, a pound for stray animals at the foot of Fair Hill.

Prior to 1850 the law was upheld locally by two elected parish constables, the first jail or 'kitty' being three cells under the stables of the Angel Inn in King's Arms (Thirlwalls) Lane. In the 1830s a local writer noted that 'the constable was selected from the deafest, blindest and lamest of the inhabitants'.

Alston was slow to respond to the 1843 Act of Parliament concerning 'The Appointment and Payment of Parish Constables'. A petition to the county requesting the provision of a Lock-up House with cells 'for persons not yet committed for trial', was finally made in 1847.

The Lock-up was built by Francis Davidson of Haydon Bridge at a cost of around £700. The first stone was laid on 12 June 1849, and the new constable – probably George Martin of Whitehaven (then aged 36) – began work on 4 May 1850. A travelling tinker, apprehended the following day, was the first offender to be incarcerated in the 'elegant edifice'.

By 1860 the building was being described as the Police Station and comprised 'a well built residence for a constable (one of the county constabulary), together with a lock-up for prisoners [three cells] and a room for magisterial business, petty sessions etc.'. The magistrates sat once a month. Seen here with its garden freshly landscaped, the Police Station was usually run by a resident sergeant and one constable, both of whom feature in the photograph. They are wearing 'Court Dress' uniform of helmet, badged belt and white gloves.

Sgt. Thomas Atkinson Farrer (b.1860, Shap), seen on the steps with his wife Mary (b.1857, Paddington, London), lived on the premises with his family. He took over from Sgt. Robert Hodgson. Farrer transferred from Brigham, near Cockermouth, where the residents presented him with an engraved silver salver in October 1891. Both his children (standing at the pillar tap) were born there. Daughter Margaret (b.1884; d.1927, Alston) married plumber and garage owner J.H. Henderson in 1912 and son Henry, known as Harry (b.1888; d.1955, Sunderland) later became a police officer.

The forge building on the left, adjoining the elevated section of road, has long since been demolished. At the time no properties had been built up the Nenthead road beyond the entrance to Jollybeard Lane.

This photograph was taken c.1899, an estimated three years after the previous one. Since then the front garden of the Police Station has flourished and children Margaret and Henry (by now aged around 14 and 11) have grown. Their father, Sgt. Farrer, stands on the steps alongside them with a constable, possibly Robert W. Davidson (b.1870, Ousby). Both are wearing regular uniform with summer 'Cheshire' style jacket, no belt and pill-box cap. The signpost at the right-hand edge reading Nenthead 4½ miles and Stanhope 21 is a new feature.

The scene is dominated by the activity in the foreground, with the final process of making a water-bound macadam road underway. Here, the binding (or 'blinding') surface coat is seen laid out on the left, waiting to be sprayed with water and rolled into a hard, smooth surface of 'bicycle-excellence' standard. The binding coat was made up of a layer of chippings (whinstone preferred) and dust of up to 2 inches.

Mechanical traction later sounded the death knell for water- and mud-bound macadamised roads, which were gradually replaced with a variety of 'tarred macadam' and later concrete alternatives. These were first introduced in busy urban areas, but many country districts continued with the old 'metalling' techniques for several decades.

Here the water bouser is being driven by John Place (aged 65), farmer and carter of Low Skelgill and father of Thomas (seen on page 10). The steamroller was made by Marshall & Sons of Gainsborough. To its left are several workmen and a bowler-hatted official, possibly district road surveyor John William Kirsopp (b.1869, Alston). Previously a roadman, Kirsopp took over from his father (also John) when he died in 1895. John junior resigned in 1900 and went to work for Carlisle Council. His successor in Alston was another ex-roadman, Joseph William Roddam (b.1862, Garrigill), who also became Sanitary Inspector c.1920 and served for about 30 years. The 1901 census shows 12 'road surfacemen' living in Alston. The youngest of these was Robert 'Bobby' Hodgson (22), also seen on page 10, and the eldest John Martin, aged 68.

Sgt. Farrer, who was succeeded by Joseph Dockray, retired in 1902, aged 42, and was presented with 'a purse of gold, containing over £40' by the people of Alston. His early discharge was due to ill health – a reoccurrence of injuries caused by an assault at Cockermouth in 1888. By 1910 he had purchased Laburnum Cottage, nearly opposite the Police Station. He lived there for many years and died in 1933, aged 73, at Sunderland, where his son Henry was a police inspector.

Unveiling Ceremony of Alston War Memorial Sept 4th 1922

This procession had gathered outside the Police Station above Victoria Square at Townhead on Monday 4 September 1922 for the unveiling of the War Memorial. It was reported to be 'one of the few real summer days of the year'.

The town band led the procession to the memorial site at the junction of the Penrith and Brampton roads. A group of ex-servicemen followed the band, marshalled under Captain Lawson, assistant master at Samuel King's School (SKS). Behind them were the district council, clergy, schoolchildren and townspeople.

The obelisk that commemorates Alston's war dead is made of Westmorland limestone on a Penrith red sandstone base and was constructed by C. Parkin & Son of Crosby Ravensworth. Measuring over 18 feet high, it is dedicated to the 37 men and one woman (Alice Renwick of the Women's Army Auxiliary Corps) who died in the Great War. The site, on part of the Raise Estate, was gifted by Isaac Walton, who also contributed £300 towards its cost. Lord Lonsdale, the Lord Lieutenant, was chosen to carry out the unveiling as many of those named on the memorial (and attending the ceremony) had served with the 'Lonsdale Battalion' of the Border Regiment. The Revd Harvey Royse RN dedicated the obelisk, and speeches were made by Alston-born R.H. Millican (Lord Mayor of Newcastle) and Major General Sir C. Lowther MP.

Wreaths were also laid in St Augustine's Church at the beautiful oak war memorial chancel screen. This was erected in 1920, the church's golden jubilee year, at a cost of about £550. Two of the panels name those who fell.

The Nenthead road, seen in the centre of the picture, originally passed over a humpback bridge at this point. The bridge still exists and lies about 12 feet below the road's present level. It crossed the Overburn mill race, which flowed from Fair Hill (to the right) down past the forge buildings to the left. The rear of these now lie below ground level.

Alston War Memorial.

UNVEILING

by

THE RIGHT HON.

The Earl of Lonsdale,

Lord Lieutenant of Cumberland,

of the

OBELISK

at **ALSTON**, erected to the memory of those who gave their lives in the Great War, 1914 to 1918.

Councillor SAMUEL LEE will preside.

MONDAY, 4th SEPT., 1922, at 3-30 p.m.

T. W. TATTERS, PRINTER, ALSTON.

A 1910 photograph showing the upstairs rear portion of the forge and blacksmiths seen in the previous picture. This was built on the west bank of the Overburn mill race and was later extended eastwards with the stream culverted beneath the ground floors. Structurally a two-storey building, the foreground area has been infilled, with the forge below accessed from the other side. The property on the right has long since been demolished.

An overshot 14-foot diameter water wheel was used to operate a tilt-hammer and other machinery. The wheel was located in a walled ground floor pit (out of view at lower left) and fed with water from a branch that led off the main race, under the police station yard. Sluices there could be opened to provide water for street cleaning when the forge and mills were not operating. Since its abandonment as a utility, the mill race has been associated with long-term flooding problems. Repiping of the upper sections was carried out in 1980.

Many generations of the Little family have lived and worked here as blacksmiths, whitesmiths and ironmongers, possibly as far back as 1700. The family name was variously spelled Liddle, Litl, Lietel – and later Litell up to c.1860. Census returns describe this property as 'Little's Buildings', while surviving invoices show they produced a wide range of domestic, farming and mining goods. Products included tools, cart and carriage parts, and 'Glendinning' kitchen ovens, which are still to be found in some old properties today.

Seen here from the left are Thomas Bell, John Little (father, aged 55), Louis (son, 24), John (grandson, 2), Mark Douglas (17, with Miss Blackett-Ord's donkey), Arthur Henderson (from Nent Hall, 21) shoeing, and farmer Teasdale Lowe (Hill House, 68) with his work horse.

After his father John (b.1855) retired, Louis Little operated the business during the 1920s, followed by Tom Bell up to the second war. John's elder brother Joseph (b.1842), originally a blacksmith, later qualified (MRCVS) and practised for many years as a veterinary surgeon. He lived at Townhead opposite the forge. Edwin (b.1885), his son and assistant, was also a vet. He worked in London before returning to Alston. Both were district veterinary inspectors.

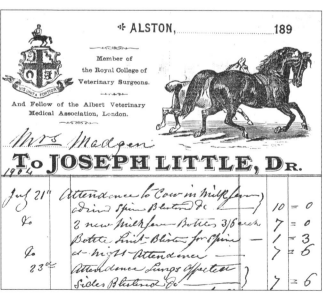

Invoice, 1904

Lorne (Lawn) House and cottage occupies an elevated position close to the forge at the head of Overburn (also known as Back o' the Burn). John Little the blacksmith and Mrs Davison (wife of Thomas) are seen in their respective gardens c.1912.

The town map of 1775 shows no properties above the old grammar school, nor any to the east across the burn. This area later contained a quaint collection of cottages and business premises, mostly built during the first part of the nineteenth century.

In 1797 a second, larger Wesleyan Methodist Chapel was built on a new site at the lower end of Overburn on its east side. This closed in 1867 and was converted into two houses. From there about ten further properties were built, some with outside stairs, ending with the ones seen on the left of the picture. When the photograph was taken the row comprised six cottages; a house with a barn, coach house and warehouse owned by Hannah Stephenson; and a stable used by Michael Brough, the (upper) slaughterhouse-man. The small, mainly commercial premises on the opposite side included storerooms, stables, several workshops, three slaughterhouses, a candle factory, smithy and joinery shop with sawpit and yard (the latter opposite Lorne House). The long-established tallow candle business was operated by Dickinson & Co. from c.1805 to the 1880s and was a major supplier to the lead mines.

From the 1850s (and in records up to WWII), three generations of the Irving family (Chris, John and John W.) operated as joiners, cart- and wheelwrights from premises between the old grammar school and the two lower slaughterhouses. At the time of the photograph, the latter were run by butchers Adamson Pickering (who succeeded J.J. Shield, d.1910) whose shop was in the Market Place, and Joseph Hodgson, who had a shop adjoining Spring House, Townfoot. Most of these properties remain intact, although in a different guise. The lower slaughterhouse, which operated for over a century until the late 1940s, still contains original equipment.

The Overburn, which was harnessed as a mill race, initially flowed in an open channel from a small early dam near the left of the picture. The larger, later mill race was culverted through the centre of Back o' the Burn to the old chapel, where a branch diverted water to the High Mill. It is possible that at an earlier period the main road into the town ran through this area, as the fresh water supply from Fair Hill did at a later date.

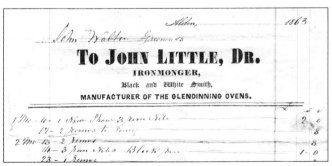

Invoice, 1863

This print from a glass negative shows the new Samuel King's School (County Council Secondary mixed) under construction in 1908, with 27 posed workmen ('tradesmen' in white aprons) along with their 'gaffer', who is wearing a bowler hat.

The 1902 Balfour Education Act empowered local authorities to provide both elementary and secondary education, thereby replacing the old School Boards. Following the closure of the grammar school c.1900, the decision was taken to build a new secondary school. Money from four existing charitable sources was pooled and a scheme prepared in 1906.

The principal sum of £2,000 had been left to the town in 1872 by Samuel King of Glasgow (d.1878), in memory of his mother's birthplace. This money was reserved for 'higher education' by the Charity Commissioners, and by the time the school was proposed had accrued to £2,875. Together with the Fair Hill (1739), Rob. Burne (1865) and John Cowper (1868) Funds, the resources available totalled £3,360, yielding an annual income of £140. After negotiations with the governors, the County Council agreed to build and furnish a new secondary school costing up to £4,000, with Alston contributing the annual charity income towards its upkeep. The 2.1 acre site at Bankfoot, near Townhead, was donated by Mr R.H. Horrocks of Little Salkeld Hall.

The new secondary school was only the fourth in Cumberland. Originally, the opening ceremony was planned for 14 September 1909, with J.W. Lowther, House of Commons Speaker and local MP officiating. However, the date was changed to 26 October with Lord Morpeth doing the honours. In the event he was substituted 'on the morning' by his wife, Lady Morpeth. She was presented with the gold key (inscribed to her husband!) by architect T. Taylor Scott.

Built of local sandstone by J. Birkett at a cost of about £3,600, the school was described as an 'excellent structure and massively built … an ornament to the neighbourhood'. It took mixed pupils from the age of ten and was designed to accommodate 55 to 60 children. Opening with 46 scholars – 27 boys and 19 girls – the average attendance was c.50.

Although offering scholarship places (twelve on opening), the school was fee-paying, with annual charges initially set at £6. Later they rose to £10/15s, but were reduced back to £6 in the late 1920s due to local hardship. The school was managed by twelve governors, with headmaster Mr H.W. Cousins supported by three teachers, a cookery instructor and a woodwork assistant. For many years the latter was Tom Kearton, a member of the firm shown in the photograph doing the joinery work. Soon after the school opened, Mr Cousins was succeeded by the long-serving James McIntosh.

Samuel King's School moved to larger premises in 1957, after which the original building was refurbished by Kearton's at a cost of £11,250, reopening as a primary school in 1960.

Nearly 130 years after his death, little has been written about the identity and life of Samuel King, the original benefactor of the school that bears his name. His grandfather, also Samuel, was a Glasgow wright who married Ann Hamilton in 1763. They had six children, including Andrew (born on 23 March 1784) who was the father of Samuel King.

In 1813 Andrew became a member of the Burgess & Guild Brethren of Glasgow, and by 1820 was trading as a cotton spinner (Andrew King & Co.). The family lived on the corner of West Carleton Place in the Gorbals, facing the River Clyde, and were later described as 'power loom cloth manufacturers' with factories at North Albion Street and Cowcaddens Road.

On 15 September 1817, Andrew married Sarah Ann Hutchinson in Alston, perhaps after visiting or working at Alston cotton and flax mill (later woollen mill). She was the daughter of Sarah Ann Richardson (b.1762) of Nunwick Hall and Randalholme. Her father was William Hutchinson (b.1759) of Alston.

Andrew and Sarah Ann had five children, the first three of whom died in infancy. The youngest survivor was Samuel, born on 26 December 1827. Andrew, his father, died in January 1839, aged 54, of 'decline', having set up a most precise will and trust fund (dated 4 July 1832) to support his wife and surviving children until they were 21. Only Samuel survived to inherit the property and cash (c.£2,200) that his father left. His mother, Sarah Ann, had died in July 1838 of consumption aged 50.

Records indicate that Samuel remained in Glasgow, where in 1841, aged 13, he was a student living with his teacher, Miss McLaren. In 1851 he is described as an 'annuitant' (possibly receiving trust fund income) living with his aunt Janet Carswell (his father's sister). The 1871 census records 43-year-old Samuel as a 'portioner', or owner of a divided piece of land, living with his second cousin Barbara C. Hardie.

In May 1871 he bought his own house at 24 Newton Place, off Sauchiehall Street, for £1,900. The scant evidence available suggests that he did not follow a profession or enter business, and was not involved in public or civic life. Later on his income was largely derived from share investments. Samuel travelled abroad (he was in Paris in 1861), occasionally visited Alston, and read a lot. He rented Claddoch Cottage in Dunoon (near where his cousin lived) and died there on 15 July 1878 after being ill for a week with peritonitis. Despite requesting to be buried 'anywhere convenient to the place of my decease' (although not in the Gorbals where his parents and siblings were) his body was taken back to Glasgow by boat.

His estate was mainly made up of stocks and shares amounting to about £21,000, largely invested in railway companies. Under his 1872 will, this was administered by seven trustees, all of whom received a 'small' legacy, with £500 each left to two male second cousins. The total value of his personal estate was £22,387, including a one-sixth share (valued at £350) in Howgillrigg Farm, Alston, which he inherited from his mother. This sum excluded the value of his house at 24 Newton Place which he left under a life interest tenancy ('liferent') to three female second cousins.

Under his 'Alston Bequest', Samuel left £2,000 sterling to the town of Alston, 'being my mother's native place … paid over to the Magistrates or Corporation or Municipal Authorities … to be applied by them to such objects, whether charitable, educational, or otherwise as shall appear to them most likely to be a benefit to the said town'.

Problems arose when it became apparent that it was, 'not a Municipal Town or Burgh and had no Chief Magistrate limited to itself'. Although there was a local magistrates bench, the Samuel King trustees expressed concerns about their ability to administer the bequest, and being fearful of counter-claims decided to take counsel's opinion in November 1878. This advice involved the eminent QC William Pearson, in consultation with the Lord Advocate and others, and cost £32/11/5d. After much correspondence the legal experts recommended that, with the consent of Alston's magistrates and Poor Law Guardians, the money be paid to the Official Trustees of Charitable Funds at the Bank of England. A letter of 3 October 1879 confirmed that £1,800 (£2,000 less duty of 10 per cent) had been invested in the purchase of £1,836/14/8d consolidated £3 per cent [sic] annuities in the name of the official trustees. Eventually, after a number of setbacks, Alston received its rightful inheritance, and the sum accrued interest for nearly 30 years until a suitable project was found. Local suggestions for how to spend the money in 1878 were: rebuilding the Market Cross; removing old buildings; paying for well paved streets; providing a piped water supply and … building a new grammar school!

Samuel King left the remainder of his estate, amounting to about £20,000, to the Merchants House of Glasgow, a charitable institution of which he became a member (No. 3,640) in 1870, aged 43. He was interred in their burial ground at the Necropolis ('City of the Dead') on 19 July 1878.

Samuel King's grave (ctr)

His monument by J.&G. Mossman is a decorated Celtic cross, measuring about 14 feet high, on a deep base. It is made of fine silver-grey granite and cost £150, plus £16 extra for kerbs. This stands on the hilltop Zeta section (grave 76) of the cemetery, with superb views over Glasgow. The cross is inscribed: 'Samuel King, a man greatly beloved, died 15th July 1878 in the 51st year of his age'. Carving on the base reads: 'In lasting memory and grateful acknowledgement of the munificent liberality of Mr. Samuel King under whose settlement the Merchants House of Glasgow received upwards of twenty thousand pounds sterling, the Directors of the House resolve to preserve and uphold this monument in time coming'. The total cost of his funeral arrangements, including a double coffin with 'best gold mountings' was £393/2/3d.

Samuel King never married, had no children and appears to have had few close family connections, except the cousins named in his will. Considering the size of his fortune, he made relatively little provision for them, with the vast majority of his estate being bequeathed for charitable purposes.

This unusual rear view of the Ruth Lancaster James Cottage Hospital was taken *c.*1912 looking west towards Raise and Park Fell. The hospital was designed by T. Taylor Scott of Carlisle, who also planned Samuel King's School. The female ward is to the left (south), with the male ward to the right; both had washroom/toilet facilities. The projecting portion contained the kitchen, office and staff room.

The Rural District Council was asked to provide a district hospital following the Alston smallpox outbreak of July and August 1902. An Isolation Hospital Committee was formed and unsuccessfully explored sites for a new facility. Options that were rejected included a local building at High Shield Hill and a joint venture with Haltwhistle Council at Coanwood.

Mrs R.L. James (née Dickinson, b.1824, Alston) who lived in Liverpool but retained close links with Alston, had in the past 'liberally subscribed to local charitable needs', including settling the Fairhill Recreation Ground debt. She was dissuaded from erecting free cottage homes for the elderly in favour of a cottage hospital, which could also provide early treatment for injured mine and quarry workers. Finalised in spring 1906, her £5,000 endowment, as well as purchasing the 3 acre site at 'Townhead Field', was used to build, equip and later partly maintain the new hospital. This incorporated the latest lighting, heating, ventilation and sanitary arrangements (including 'flush toilets') and cost £2,026. Sadly, Mrs James died in April 1907 before the ten-bed, two-cot hospital was completed.

When opened by Lady Mabel Howard on 23 June 1908, patients had to pay fees, although there was a subscription scheme in place. Outpatient care and home nursing were also available. Dr Stewart Carson was the first medical officer, supported by Miss C. Davidson as matron.

In 1926 the 'Recommend Scheme' of benefits was introduced. This allowed block membership through associations (eight in 1929) such as Greenwich Hospital workers, Vieille Montagne Mining Co. and Women's Institutes. It cost two guineas per week to stay at the hospital, and eleven guineas for an operation.

In September 1929 the 'New Wing' was opened by Miss Maud Drake of London, a member of the Dickinson family and relative of Mrs James. Some of the £1,200 required was raised by public subscription, and fundraising began in 1928 with a £200 donation from Isaac Walton. The extension contained an X-ray department and an operating theatre dedicated to Dr S. Carson Jr. He had been born in Nenthead in 1858 and practised locally for 44 years, dying in 1925 aged 66. His father, who had the same name, practised as a surgeon at Nenthead from 1842–66 and at Alston from 1866–88. By the time of his death in 1888, aged 79, he had completed 46 years service. According to records, both father and son 'died in harness'.

Although the hospital is now surrounded by a school and houses on three sides, the superb westerly view still remains. There is also still a portrait of Mrs James in the main corridor, presented by her friend and executor, George W. Mumford.

Ruth Lancaster Dickinson came from a prominent Alston family. Her grandfather John, followed by his eldest son Thomas (her uncle) were Moormasters, controlling the valuable mines and minerals on the Greenwich Hospital's *c*.22,000 acre Alston Moor estate. John and his wife Mary moved from Annat Walls to Lowbyer in 1790 when he was engaged as Moormaster (he retired in 1825). Ruth's father Joseph,

the third son of nine children, was born there in April 1795.

In October 1823, when he was twenty-eight, Joseph married Ruth Rowell, daughter of Nicholas and Agnes Rowell (née Lancaster), at Alston. Their only child, Ruth Lancaster Dickinson, was baptised on 26 August 1824. Her father, who was described at the time as 'a surveyor of landed estates and mines' (he employed the famous Thomas Sopwith) was also noted as a 'spirit dealer' and by 1828 as a 'tallow chandler'.

Ruth's mother died in 1831, aged thirty-nine, when she was only seven, after which she was brought up by her father at what is now No. 4 Townfoot. She later travelled widely and may have visited America. Joseph continued to work as a land surveyor until his death in 1853, aged 58, and is buried with his wife in St Augustine's churchyard. Ruth stayed at Townfoot where the 1861 census records her as a 'landed proprietor'. She continued to travel and was probably well known to wealthy Daniel James, as she was one of three female guests at his home when the 1871 census was taken (together with his three teenage sons and five servants). Daniel, a widower aged 68, and Ruth, a spinster of 46, were married at St Augustine's Church, Alston, on 5 July 1871.

Her substantial wealth is explained by her husband's background. Daniel was born into a British immigrant family in New York in 1803, marrying Elizabeth Phelps, daughter of New York entrepreneur Anson Phelps, in 1829. He later became a junior partner in US metals, mining and trading giant Phelps, Dodge & Co., and as the company supplied English customers with cotton (returning with tin, iron, copper etc.),

he moved to Liverpool with Elizabeth in 1831, where three of their four children were born. After she died in 1847, aged 39, he remained in Liverpool where he was recorded as an 'American merchant (metal trade)'. He then married Sophia Hitchcock from New York and had three sons.

In 1867 and by now a British subject, he purchased the impressive Beaconsfield Estate (*c*.12 acres) at Little Woolton, Liverpool for £11,862. Sophia died there in 1870, aged 50, and the following year he married Ruth L. Dickinson. Daniel died five years later, in November 1876, aged 73, leaving assets of £45,000 in England.

Ruth, who retained several Alston properties, including Harbut Law farm and house, which bears a plaque on the porch reading 'RLJ 1879', continued to live at Beaconsfield until her death, aged 82, on 4 April 1907. She left £56,300 and was buried in the nearby churchyard of All Saints, Childwall, where her modest gravestone includes the words 'Born at Alston, Cumberland', 'Died at her residence Beaconsfield' and 'She hath done what she could'.

The Phelps, Dodge Corporation was one of the world's largest copper mining and manufacturing groups and was founded in 1834 by Anson Phelps and junior partners sons-in-law William Dodge and Daniel James. It began as an export, import and trading company, later expanding into timber, mining and manufacturing. By 1859 Daniel held a 28 per cent share of the $1.5m business. In 1908, the enlarged corporation, capitalised at $45m, employed nearly 8,000 people.

Harbut Law, Alston, *c*.1910

Beaconsfield House at Little Woolton was demolished *c*.1930 to build 'superior' modern houses

Porch with plaque (RLJ 1879) at Harbut Law

Town Head, Alston

A *c*.1907 view looking up Front Street towards the Victoria Square area at Townhead. To the left, fronted with cobbles, is the old Grammar School, with the Swan's Head Hotel in the centre and St Paul's Church (Wesleyan Methodist) to the right.

The Grammar School, possibly founded in the late sixteenth century, was rebuilt by subscription in 1828, as the stone plaque above the door testifies. It was supported by a small endowment from the Fairhill Trust (£45 in 1897) plus an annual grant of £10 from the Greenwich Hospital. There were no free places, but fees were limited to a 'moderate' sum. Built for 80 pupils, numbers had dwindled to 30 by 1897, and the school closed *c*.1900 when headmaster George Davies retired, aged 65. Born at Pembroke Dock, he gave 40 years service.

In this picture the former school has been converted to a grocery shop, which was run by ex co-op manager Thomas Pickering until *c*.1935 when it was briefly acquired by Donald Robson. Later purchased by the Co-op, it was requisitioned during the war by the National Fire Service, then sold to Cumberland County Council as a permanent fire station in the 1950s.

The Swan's Head (not to be confused with the Swan Inn near the Market Place, which closed *c*.1899) became a public house in about 1860 and was run for over 30 years by Teasdale Haldon and later his son John. Following three short lets, it was occupied by Richard Fearnley by the time this postcard was produced. He acted as manager for the Brampton Brewery Co. and was succeeded shortly afterwards by the long-serving John Beeby. The grocery shop next door belonged to the Pickering family, at this time Mary and Hannah.

St Paul's was the third Wesleyan chapel to be built in Alston. The large, extravagant Italianate style building dominates the skyline and represents the peak period of Wesleyan Methodist influence. Opened in April 1868

to accommodate 600, it was designed by R.F.N. Haswell of North Shields and built by Thomas Cranston. The cost of £2,500 was raised by public subscription, the fittings including a 'fine organ by Nicholson of Carlisle'. This building replaced the 1797 chapel at Back o' the Burn. It is built of pale sandstone with striking red and yellow ashlar decorations, twin arched front doors and an abundance of large gallery windows. A spacious school room and caretaker's house was added as late as 1933. The railings of Hundy Hall (by now two properties) are seen to the right.

Advert, *Carlisle Journal*, 5 October 1866

Advert, 1912

An early 1920s view of upper Front Street, taken from the gable end of the Quaker Meeting House (on the immediate left). Below Martin Tindle's two shops is the portico entrance of the 'new' bank. The large double fronted drapery store opposite belonged to Thomas Arthur Holmes, but always traded as Simpson & Son. On the right, with its shopfront facing downhill, is the grocers formerly owned by Hannah Stephenson, which was occupied by William Reece when this picture was taken.

Although never a large group, Quakers had established themselves in the area by the late seventeenth century and were most active from 1720–70. The first meeting house was erected on this site in 1732, as confirmed by a dated lintel above the door. In 1764 the roof was raised and a gallery installed. In spite of declining membership, the meeting house was restored c.1860, the balcony removed, new larger windows inserted and a porch added. The 1732 lintel stone was resited as part of this work. After Quaker meetings ceased in 1902, the building was used by the Rechabites until the 1930s, then became the Toc H group centre. The Quakers returned in the late 1970s and the building was refurbished in 1996.

Martin Tindle was born at Greenhead in 1846, although his parents came from Longbenton in Newcastle. His father Matthew was an 'enginesmith' at Alston's railway station workshops. Martin opened the lower shop c.1875 as a druggists, but quickly became a grocer and drysalter (selling dried meats, pickles, etc). Later, assisted by his son Matthew Henry (b.1876, Alston), he took on the adjoining premises, which are seen here filled with toys and games. A sign reading 'Pretty & Useful Presents' is displayed across the window (with metal spikes along the cill!). Tindle also sold tennis racquets, walking sticks and his own range of postcards. Henry, a Rural District Councillor, later ran the business for many years, helped by his wife Mary Olive, daughter of miller Joseph Lancaster.

The archway below the gas lamp led to several properties at the rear, including a bakery and private school prior to 1850. Originally called Bakehouse Lane, then Pattinson Close, it had become West View by the 1890s. Henry lived at the rear, while his father Martin lived above the shops.

The rather elaborate, red sandstone building (with railings) beyond had been rebuilt for the Carlisle & Cumberland Bank in 1898. By this time it was a branch of Liverpool & Martins Bank.

Adverts: top 1894; bottom 1888

This rare view of the former 'Carlisle & Cumberland Branch Bank Ltd.' on Front Street dates from c.1895. The archway of West View is to the left, with another passageway (possibly Smith's Lane) to the right, abutting Hugh Walton's shop and house. The Carlisle & Cumberland Banking Company was established in Lowther Street, Carlisle, in 1836. James Millican of Alston became a local agent in 1869, but had to provide a bond of £4,000 to secure the agency, for which he was paid a salary of £80 p.a. The following letter, dated 17 February 1869, suggests that the Alston branch originally adjoined Millican's draper's shop two doors down: 'On the recommendation of Bainbridge & Millican [Solicitors, Alston] I am inclined to apply for the agency. Should you decide to open a branch and consider my application favourably, terms could be arranged afterwards. I have premises adjoining my place of business quite suitable for a Bank and in an excellent situation … James Millican.'

James's older brother John took over the bank c.1873, having returned from Newcastle to resume business in Alston, but by 1879 the agency had been transferred to George Peart. He was also a land agent and county court bailiff, and ran the bank from the refurbished premises seen here, with modern shop façade and accommodation ('Bank House') above.

In 1883 Peart was succeeded as manager by teacher Robert Elliot (b.1855, Alston), who is seen on the right of this photograph. After acquiring Hugh Walton's adjoining property, the flourishing bank completely rebuilt its Alston branch in 1898 at a cost of £4,450. During the work the Elliots temporarily moved to Lovelady Shield. The much enlarged and rather ostentatious new building features a cornucopia of architectural detail, including several decorative panels and a replica date stone reading 'IDF: 1727'. It also incorporated the new Bank House.

In 1882 Robert (the brother of auctioneer Adam Elliot) married Sarah J. Thompson, whose family traded as druggists in the Market Place for about sixty years. Following Robert's death in 1916, aged 61, he was succeeded as bank manager by his son George Thompson Elliot (b.1885, Alston). George, who began work as a bank clerk in 1900, aged 15, is seen on the left of this photograph.

George Thompson – described as 'a man of many interests' – was also a poultry farmer at Potter's Lonnen, a stocking factory operator, local Methodist preacher and JP. He retired in 1945 after forty-five years employment (c.30 as manager) and died in 1959, aged 74. Father and son both lived at Bank House and gave 78 years combined service, including 63 as managers. During this period a series of mergers and name-changes saw the Carlisle & Cumberland become the Bank of Liverpool (1911), Liverpool & Martins (by 1920) and shortly afterwards just Martins. Since c.1960 it has been Barclays Bank.

The jumbled maze of narrow lanes and small squares made some parts of old Alston difficult to photograph. Problems caused by confined spaces, restricted light and dark shadows were made worse when shooting uphill into a bright sky. All these obstacles were overcome by Thomas Bramwell in this sharp c.1894 view, which also features sixteen motionless people. It was taken looking up Front Street through the top 'narrows' towards the Swan's Head Inn (whose sign shows Thomas Davison as landlord).

In the foreground is a close-up of H. Walton's odd-shaped bay window, which blocked the pavement at this point. Hugh Walton was an ironmonger, plumber and tinsmith, and the window is filled with oil lamps, china, ornaments and pictures. His father Joseph was a tinplate worker, born in Dorset c.1810, who was based in Alston from the 1840s. In 1871 the family were living at the gasworks where son William (b.1843) was manager for nearly 20 years from c.1870–90. In August 1890 William emigrated to Australia to join brother John, dying there in August 1895.

Joseph died in 1876, aged 67, after which his wife Jane (d.1883, aged 70) took over the business, assisted by sons John (b.1853) and Hugh (b.1860), both tinsmiths. They established the shop seen here c.1880. Hugh, the youngest of the seven children, carried on the business after his mother's death and John's departure to Australia in 1886, marrying Maria Craig in 1883. She died after daughter Maria's birth in 1889 (Maria married Joseph Pratt, mineral water manufacturer of Rodsley House, in 1911).

In about 1897, with the impending demolition of these premises to make way for a new and enlarged bank, Hugh moved to Thirlwall Storey's nearby shop in the Potato Market, where he remained until his death in 1928, aged 69. His second wife Isabella (née Lupton) continued the company for a few years assisted by daughter May (b.1908) before selling to John Harrison Nicholson. As well as being an ironmonger, a staunch Congregationalist and a keen angler, Hugh Walton later became a skilful photographer, specialising in outdoor and landscape views.

The double fronted shop on the left was home to 'Simpson & Son – Drapers and Clothiers'. This was one of the oldest businesses in Alston, having been established in 1822 by William Simpson (born Alston c.1801) as a drapers and grocers. After his death in 1844, wife Mary ran the business, later assisted by sons Thomas (b.1834) and William Johnson (b.1837).

Mary died in 1876, aged 70, and William (seen on the left) was in charge from c.1873, expanding the business to include outfitting, tailoring and hat departments. An original member of the Rural District Council, he died in January 1897, aged 59. After that the shop was run by his wife Mary (born Allenheads c.1849). She is seen on her husband's left, with an assistant (possibly Bill Holmes) beyond holding a parcel. Daughter Dora (born 1873 and the eldest of six siblings) married Thomas Arthur Holmes (b.1870, Grassfield, Nenthead; farmer and land agent) in 1901 and took over the business. Thomas was later vice chairman of the Rural District Council, County

Councillor, JP and governor of Samuel King's School. He died in 1926, aged 55. For nearly sixty years the shop was then run by his son 'Willie' Walton Holmes (b.1902). It was taken over by a nephew in 1983 and continued to trade until the early 1990s, still retaining the Simpson name.

'Bank View', seen centre, was established as a grocery and bakery business *c.*1892 by the industrious Hannah Stephenson (left of the doorway). Later on it was altered to include double side and front shop windows. Stern-looking but of 'genial disposition and obliging nature', widowed Hannah (née Varty, b.1849 Dryburn, Garrigill) is seen here with three of her four children, Jane Ann (b.1874) left, Jason (b.1890) and Emma (b.1877). Hannah later set up the nearby Victoria Temperance Hotel, which she operated until her death in November 1919 after eight years of illness (son John George died in May 1919, aged 23). She supplemented her expanded provisions and bakery business by taking in lodgers, the 1901 census showing seven, mainly tradesmen involved in constructing the Victoria. One of these, Joseph Gladstone (aged 20, plumber, Gateshead) married her daughter Emma. After Hannah's death, the grocery and bakery business was acquired by William Reece.

RICHARD HENRY MILLICAN (1854–1933)

Educated at Alston Grammar School and Gosberton Hall, Lincs, Richard Millican later lived in Newcastle upon Tyne. He took an active interest in athletics and rowing, and was president of several football, swimming and bowling clubs, as well as Newcastle Rotary Club and the Cumberland & Westmorland Association. Richard Millican was elected: Newcastle City Councillor 1904; JP 1906; Sheriff of Newcastle 1910; Alderman 1921; Lord Mayor 1921/22; and Deputy Lord Mayor 1928/29 (the year of the 'North East Coast Exhibition'). In addition, he was chairman of the Watch Committee (Police & Fire Departments), the Liberal Club and various Wesleyan Methodist groups, as well as a governor of the Royal Victoria Infirmary and a member of the Council of Armstrong College. Alston Rural District Council held an honorary luncheon for him as Lord Mayor of Newcastle, with Lady Mayoress Rita Millican (his daughter), at the Town Hall on 7 September 1922. He died in January 1933, aged 78. His company, Reed, Millican Ltd. was taken over by Pilkington Bros. *c.*1960.

This animated view was taken from the Potato Market looking up Front Street towards Townhead *c.*1895. The two roadmen, one with a 'whacker', are relaying stone cobbles which were used to pave both market places and many of the town's main streets.

The imposing top-hatted figure on the left is probably John Millican (b.1822, Tynehead). In 1844, after serving a draper's apprenticeship (living in) with the Simpson family, he established the drapery business that occupied the double fronted shop on the right (facing the Simpsons).

In the mid-1860s John moved to Newcastle to become a glass merchant, in association with his brother-in-law, Joseph Reed. At that point his brother James Millican (b.1829) took over the Alston business and in 1871 was described as a 'draper with four apprentices'.

John later became a partner in Reed, Millican & Co., glass and paint merchants of Newcastle, but returned to his Alston shop (probably by 1873) with at least five of his eleven children. He continued to trade as a draper until his retirement *c.*1887. Subsequently a JP, vice-chairman of the Rural District Council and a steward for the Wesleyan chapels circuit, he died in March 1901 aged 79.

The business was continued by his son, John Holmes Millican (b.1852, Alston) for over 40 years until his death in March 1928, aged 76, although the company name was retained long after that. He was described as 'a leading trader' and 'pillar of the Wesleyan church'.

John senior's third son Richard Henry (b.1854, Alston)

was the most eminent member of the family. He settled in Newcastle, where he later became Lord Mayor, and was also a partner in Reed, Millican & Co. eventually becoming managing director (see previous page).

Beyond Millican's is the bay window of Hugh Walton's ironmonger's shop, and adjoining that the original premises of the Carlisle & Cumberland Bank. The rebuilding and extension of the bank in 1898 necessitated the purchase and demolition of Walton's property.

The premises of Thirlwall Storey ('Chemist and Druggist'), seen on the left, were part of a detached block that included the large double shop of Simpson & Son, out of view behind. Sandwiched between the two was a small grocer's shop and house which was run by Matthew and Elizabeth Graham when the photograph was taken. Later (*c.*1909–20) it was occupied by knit hosiery manufacturer and retired postmaster Henry Lupton (d.1920, aged 88, father of Isabella Walton).

By this time the old Queen's Head Inn, further up Front Street on the left, had been converted into two properties, the lower of which was occupied by Jane Craig, a grocer who later became a baker. The building, believed to date from the mid-seventeenth century, had a chequered career as an inn, and its last period of operation ended in the early 1880s. It was later renamed Elmfield House and Cottage, with the former run in the post First World War period as bed and breakfast apartments and a butcher's shop by Mr and Mrs John Hetherington.

John Hetherington, photographed outside his butcher's shop at the south-east corner of the Potato Market c.1912. High Mill race ran beneath the cobbled surface of Back Street (later known as Pigeon Lane), which is seen to the right. This led into Chapel Square, the site of the second Wesleyan chapel, beyond which was Overburn (also known as Back o' the Burn). The three small slaughterhouses in Overburn were operated by Adamson Pickering, Joseph Hodgson and Michael Brough, and originally used the mill stream as a drain to carry away effluent until the practice was 'officially' stopped. Alston Rural District Council records from 20 May 1899 note: 'The Medical Officer for Health … Ordered that the Clerk to the County Council be informed that all the Closets and Ashpits have been cleaned and that the outlets from the Slaughter houses to the Mill Burn had been closed'. Prior to 1890, there was also a tallow candle factory nearby, run for many decades by Dickinson & Co.

This butcher's shop and the adjacent premises were owned by various members of the Dickinson family for many years. Matthew Dickinson is recorded as a butcher as early as 1829, and was succeeded by two George Dickinsons, who were father and son. John Hetherington (a Garrigill farmer) took over the business c.1909. He later moved it

to Elmfield House (part of the old Queen's Head) where it traded into the 1930s, with his wife letting rooms ('B&B'). At about the same time, John also became proprietor of the Temperance Hotel at the bottom corner of the Potato Market.

From c.1830, the adjoining property (out of view to the left) was run by the Dickinson family as a grocery store, latterly by sisters Mary and Hannah. Around 1905 it was leased to Tom Greenwell, a well-known dealer in furniture and household goods. He lived above his other store which occupied the now demolished island property at the Market Place entrance to the Butts.

Outside stairs such as the one seen here were still a common feature in Alston at the time, even though many had been removed in the early 1900s. One of the seven original cast-iron water taps in the town was located a little further up Back Street.

GEORGE DICKINSON,

BUTCHER.

MARKET PLACE, ALSTON.

Beef, Mutton, &c., first-class quality, always on hand.

Advert, 1894

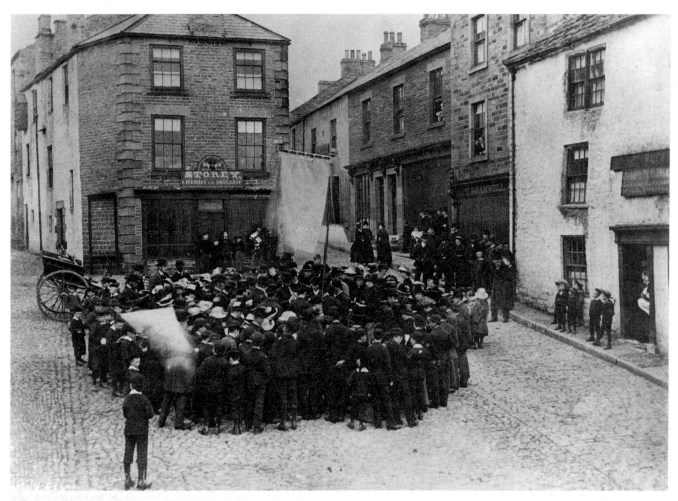

This rare view of the Potato Market with Front Street to the right may have been taken by Thomas Bramwell. His shop and house (rebuilt in the 1860s) are on the right next to the old Black Bull. This upper area was once known as the Butter Market. The unidentified group – probably a temperance or friendly society, judging by the banner – appear to be singing, accompanied by a clarinet or recorder player at the centre. The presence of many children may imply a Band of Hope meeting, while the closed window shutters suggest a Sunday. The Black Bull Inn sign shows Joseph Teasdale as innkeeper (licensee c.1882–88), suggesting the photograph was taken in the later 1880s.

Thirlwall Storey (born c.1824, Farlam) opened his chemist and grocery shop here in about 1850. The family lived in the house above and the business continued for nearly 50 years, with Hugh Walton taking over the premises c.1898.

The sign above the door, with pestle and mortar in relief, is inscribed 'Storey, Chemist and Druggist, genuine horse and cattle medicines, licensed dealer in tea, coffee, tobacco' (and game). By 1874 Thirlwall Storey was also described as a dentist, as was his son Thomas James (b.1860) from 1881. Thomas had become a 'Registered Dentist' by 1891, moving to Station Road, then relocating to Factory House (later Nentholme) by 1894. Soon after he moved to Temple Croft, where he remains in the records up to c.1914. He in turn was succeeded by his son John (born c.1888, LDS Edinburgh University) who practised at Townfoot next to 'Nana' Fortune's. Thirlwall Storey, a widower, retired to Carlisle after he sold his shop. He died in 1901, aged 77, supposedly after a tram accident. To the left of his shop is Back Street (later Pigeon Lane) which led into Chapel Square at the foot of Overburn.

The Black Bull Inn, which had been a licensed house for more than 200 years, occupied the left half of this decrepit building on the west side of Front Street, facing into the Potato Market or High Market Place. The other half was home to Samuel Proudfoot's boot and clogmaker's shop. Charles Bramwell (b.1860, Alston), who later ran the business, is probably the person standing in the doorway of his father's shop ('watchmaker, jeweller and photographer') to the left.

The Black Bull was operated for at least 40 years up to 1865 by the Watson family. William Dowson, previously at the Shaw House Inn on the Hartside to Penrith Road, took over from Joseph Teasdale c.1888. William never married and originally lived with his sister Isabella (d.1895, aged 39) and niece Hannah (m.1894 to a gypsum miner from Hunsonby). He is seen here standing at the doorway of the inn, which he continued to run until the property was demolished in 1900/01, by which time he was 63 and disappears from Alston business records. Samuel Proudfoot Jr. is also standing at the door of the premises his family had occupied since the mid-1870s. They were from Haltwhistle, where they owned another shop, and Samuel died there in 1901, aged 30.

The precise date and nature of the occasion is a matter of some conjecture. If the builder (in bowler hat), three workmen and two boys (with pick, shovel and spirit level) are about to demolish the ancient structure, then the date is 1900. However, close inspection shows the inn and shop still open, with curtains and lamps in place. The photograph may have been taken c.1893 when Thomas Bramwell extended

the back of his adjoining property to accommodate a 'large new studio' for his expanding photographic business. This involved the demolition of conjoining outbuildings and subsequent reconstruction work. Although this hypothesis seems plausible, the later arrival of Liddell & Sons, Haltwhistle ('Agricultural Implement Agents') seen on the right, would favour the c.1900 date, as would the ages of several members of the group.

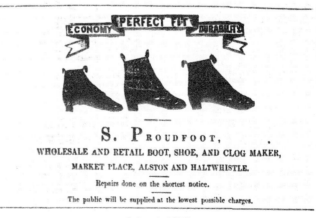

ECONOMY   PERFECT FIT   DURABILITY

S. Proudfoot,

WHOLESALE AND RETAIL BOOT, SHOE, AND CLOG MAKER,

MARKET PLACE, ALSTON AND HALTWHISTLE.

Repairs done on the shortest notice.

The public will be supplied at the lowest possible charges.

Advert, 1875

This second view shows the rear of the Black Bull, with the demolition of the washhouse? underway, along with the removal of larger outbuildings in the rear yard. The breached wall of Thomas Bramwell's property is to the right. Again, with curtains and furniture visible, it seems likely that the inn was still operating. Bearded landlord William Dowson (born *c.*1838, Alston) is in the centre, accompanied (if it is 1900) by servant Mary J. Lowe (b.1880, Alston). The bowler-hatted 'builder' – on the left with plans – is once again accompanied by his workmen. He also appears at the stone-laying ceremony for the replacement building (facing). There are few clues either to his identity or the object of this exercise, although surprisingly the photos were taken not by neighbour Thomas Bramwell, but Tom Kearton of the local building and farming family. The Black Bull was owned by John Little and records state that it was 'formerly erected by Roger Kirkpatrick'. In 1900 it was sold by Little's executors to John G. Manners, insurance manager and estate agent of West Hartlepool, who rebuilt it the following year.

Unlike the previous pictures of the Black Bull, the event taking place here is not in doubt. It is the laying of the foundation stone on 14 June 1901 of the Victoria Temperance Hotel, which replaced the dilapidated old inn.

Shortly after Alston Rural District Council was formed in December 1894, it began implementing various sections of the Public Health Acts. The local medical officer, Dr Stewart Carson, who had the power to condemn properties, began reporting on dangerous and uninhabitable buildings. It is likely that the Black Bull fell into this category in 1900. The new owner, John G. Manners, submitted redevelopment plans for the inn and adjoining premises in July that year. As part of these, he offered 'to set back the frontage of the [proposed new] premises and so widen the footpath four feet', bringing it into line with Bramwell's building. He also requested connections to the mains sewer and water pipe, while on 23 March 1901 the contractor applied 'to erect a hoarding in the street during the alterations'.

The design of the hotel was plain, functional and completely lacking in adornment. Although built of brick rather than traditional local sandstone, it emulated the latter with a cement render facing and mock-ashlar finish. Entry to the new rear courtyard and stable block was by the large archway to the left, which replaced the narrow passageway through the adjoining Bramwell building.

The connection of those noted on the commemorative plaque with Alston is not obvious. It reads 'This stone was laid by Councillor Wm. J. Coates on the 14th day of June 1901, Wm. Young Architect, Messrs Booth & Bolton Contractors, ALL OF WEST HARTLEPOOL'. Along with

others involved they were associates of the new owner John G. Manners, also of West Hartlepool, who may have had links with the Temperance movement. Other contractors were Kendry & Long, joiners (West Hartlepool), Hewitson, slater (Newcastle) and William Ferguson, plumber (Alston). Hannah Stephenson (grocer, baker and owner of apartments), later proprietress of the new hotel, is seen at the foot of the centre ladder. The 1901 census shows that seven of the workforce were boarding with her, including builder George Booth (38) and plumber Joseph Gladstone (20) who married her daughter Emma (at left ladder) in 1902. The enterprise was no doubt supported by Alderman William D. Stephens, a major temperance reformer, who retained a residence (The Highlands) on Alston Moor, but was ill at the time of this ceremony and died in December 1901 (see page 6).

The belated laying of the stone – delayed until the building was nearly at full height – was due to the sudden death on 10 May 1901 (aged 52) of the original elected official for the ceremony, Major Dickinson of Tower Hill.

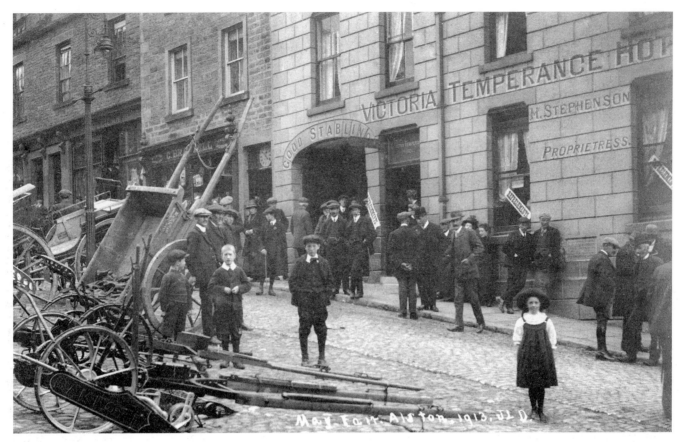

This bustling scene looking across the Potato Market towards the Victoria Temperance Hotel was taken on May Fair Day 1913. Fairs, held annually on specific days in the spring and autumn, were an important part of Alston life and centred on the sale of animals on the Fair Hill fields. The number of sales increased from three in the early part of the nineteenth century to six in the latter years, each involving different categories of livestock. Horse fairs were held along the Garrigill road near Bankfoot, where the animals could be galloped. This led to occasional reports of 'reckless accidents' or 'driving furiously'.

All the fairs were special events and attracted large crowds, with many travelling from the surrounding dales. Pre-eminent, however, was May Fair Day, held on the last Thursday in the month and taken as a holiday by most local inhabitants. The busiest event of the year, it saw all the roads into Alston filled with a continuous stream of traffic. In the town the streets thronged with people and were packed with stalls of every kind, among which were 'cheapjacks, quack doctors, Billy fair plays, minstrels, roundabouts and caravan shows'. Dancing and music were popular, and many public houses provided special entertainments in large upstairs rooms. As auction marts gradually took over from animal sales, the fairs passed into history. This moved one writer to comment: 'Held in a place apart and not in the streets of the town … lacking in conviviality, nothing for the public to see … [they are] an irreparable blow to gaiety'. Alston Moor Auction Mart was established by Adam Elliot, Samuel Walton and others in Station Road in 1918.

Widowed Hannah Stephenson, who owned the Victoria when the picture was taken, died in November 1919 and was succeeded by her daughter Emma Gladstone. She remained in charge until c.1928 when Robert Charlton took over.

Thomas Bramwell (born 1836 at Snappergill, Garrigill, the fourth of fourteen children) worked as a lead ore washer before becoming a watchmaker and jeweller. He commenced business at Alston in 1860 next to the old Queen's Head, moving several years later into the larger (and completely rebuilt) property seen here to the left of the Victoria. This building, incorporating the original alleyway beneath the clock, was believed to have been purchased by him when it was offered for sale in 1869.

Bramwell expanded the business to include spectacles, musical instruments and sewing machines, adding 'photography in all its branches' after c.1884. An original member of the Rural District Council, he was a notable photographer whose legacy appears on a wide range of postcards. When he died in 1907 aged 71, his son Charles (b.1860, Alston, formerly a merchant navy engineer, later a watchmaker) continued the business until his death in 1925, aged 64. It was then taken over by J.H. Hodgkison, 'The Chemist'. These premises probably stand on the site of the Old Dun Cow Inn ('dun' means brownish grey) which had been run, since at least 1828, by shoemaker Thomas Burn (d.1853, aged 73) and his wife Mary. After her death in December 1858, aged 76, the inn closed.

Advert, 1861

HIGH MARKET PLACE, ALSTON

This postcard view shows High Market Place (the Potato Market) and Front Street on an unusually quiet day. Hannah Stephenson's name on the Victoria Temperance Hotel indicates a pre-1920 date. Completed in 1901 with a pseudo-ashlar finish, this was one of three temperance hotels in close proximity, the others being John Hetherington's establishment on the right, and the Sun Temperance below.

The effects of temperance societies were felt as far back as the 1830s, and resulted in declining liquor sales and reduced inn rents. One such reduction at Nenthead in 1839 prompted the comment, 'Temperance Societies have ruined the trade'. Despite a largely teetotal Methodist workforce, and an abhorrence of drunkenness by major local employers such as the London Lead Company, Alston Moor supported between 25 and 30 public houses over a long period. However, many landlords derived as much profit from a range of non-alcoholic drinks as they did from liquor sales. These included coffee, soda-water, ginger beer, lemonade and black beer (a mixture of treacle and spruce fir juice). For nearly a hundred years from the 1840s, there were usually three completely teetotal temperance premises within the town, originally styled 'Temperance coffee houses'.

The butcher's shop below the Victoria with carcasses hanging outside was established in the early 1880s by William Walton (d.1926, aged 67). Also a bacon curer, sausage maker and cattle dealer, he ran the business until about 1920. He was succeeded by Alex Cairns, then Albert Biggs (1930s/40s) and later J.J. Armstrong. The premises is still a butcher's shop today. The doorway below Walton's window led to an alleyway originally called Greenwell's Lane, which provided access to several old properties to the rear. Blackett Greenwell (1806–86, Alston) started out as a joiner, then from 1840 became a noted 'animal preserver' (taxidermist), supplying specimens to private collectors and museums.

Another Walton, Thomas Richardson, operated the adjoining grocery, confectionery and tobacconist's business between c.1900 and the early 1930s. It was then taken over by Mabel (born c.1895), the daughter of John Irving Sr., joiner and cartwright. She added pies and pastries to the range of goods on offer, and some say her 'presence' remains today!

The large projecting sign indicates yet another grocer, 'Walter Willson', who appeared shortly before the First World War and remained until 1977. Their premises had previously been occupied by Harrison Hall, saddler and ironmonger.

The lower part of High Market Place showing several carts selling potatoes, each with a set of scales. The photograph was probably taken *c*.1905 and looks too quiet for a traditional Saturday market day.

These areas were extensively cobbled and carefully cambered to form 'surface' drains. The High Mill race, in an underground stone culvert, ran the length of the market place down to Crown Lane alleyway seen at centre. From there the water was originally fed in wooden trunking supported on stone pillars and brackets fixed to the rear of the buildings. In 1817 when the mill was refurbished and a new water wheel installed, this section was replaced with underground cast-iron pipes.

Crown Lane led into Sun Inn Court at its lower end near High Mill, while an easterly branch provided access to the Crown Inn stables and upper Butts area. The lane also gave entry via external stone stairways to several upstairs properties, including the offices of Chater & Atkinson, solicitors. For many years they occupied part of the old Swan Inn building lying beyond the Temperance Hotel on the left.

This latter hotel, which first appeared in local directories in about 1860, was previously one of several temperance coffee houses in the town. Originally operated by the Whitfield family, the sign shows it was in the hands of Joseph Carr when the photograph was taken. Shortly afterwards he moved to the nearby, newly opened Sun Temperance. Although 'disappearing' from the records, the Temperance Hotel continued to function, being run for many years, from about 1910, by local butcher John Hetherington.

The shop to the right of the alleyway belonged to Sarah Richardson, 'Milliner and Fancy Draper'. In spite of its balanced appearance, it was an irregular shaped building, being connected to other properties on three sides. Sarah Richardson started her business *c*.1878 aged only eighteen, and retired early in about 1913 (she died in 1938, aged 77). Her replacement, Alfred Bales of the Royal Oak Inn, continued to operate as a draper until *c*.1960, when sadly all these buildings were demolished.

An Edwardian photograph of the bottom corner of the Potato Market, showing the Royal Oak, Post Office and Crown Hotel. The Post Office, set between the two inns, was fronted by a stepped and railed patio area, but unlike its neighbours did not include any property to the rear.

The original post office was on the north side of the lower Market Place at the entrance leading down into the Butts, known then as Post Office Lane. From the 1820s to 1860s it was operated by John Dryden from his ironmongery and newsagent business. By 1869, widow Phillis Errington, a grocer and draper (born *c*.1823, Alston) had taken over as postmistress, sharing premises with Henry Lupton on Front Street. These were located at the corner of the archway into Edmunds (later Grisdale's) Lane. By 1881 she had moved the post office back up to the Market Place, adjoining Mary Kirk (drapers) at the entrance to Mill Lane. Henry Lupton (b.1834, Wakefield) took over as postmaster *c*.1883 at his shop (the fourth and final post office site) in the Potato Market. He had run a grocery, drapery and hosiery business here for several years and later also became a stationer. A widower since 1875, he served as postmaster for more than twenty years, later assisted by daughter Isabella as 'telegraph clerk'. She was born in Alston in 1870 and married Hugh Walton in 1906. By 1909 Henry Lupton had been succeeded by Rennie Miller, who was followed within a decade by James Aitchison. Lupton continued to trade as a hosiery manufacturer until his death in 1920 aged 88.

Like the Post Office, the Royal Oak, with its distinctive front canopy, has retained its familiar appearance up to the present day. This old established inn was taken over by the Diggle family in the 1850s and remained with them until *c*.1892, when it passed to relatives John and Ann Bales. Continued by Ann after the death of her husband, the family are here seen outside the entrance, with the boy sitting on the mounting steps. The inn was popular with visiting Teesdale farmers, who gained access to the rear stables via the narrow alleyway next to the Post Office. When the inn closed *c*.1914, brother Alfred Bales took over the neighbouring drapery business from Sarah Richardson. John and Tamar Bales later converted the old inn into a boarding house.

Overleaf: This photograph shows the start of the 'great destruction' of the area between the two Market Places, *c*.1960. It was taken by Jack Sewell looking east from Front Street, with the demolished remains of the old Temperance Hotel (and basement shop below) in the foreground. The centre window in the whitewashed wall looks into Crown Lane passageway, beyond which is Alf Bales' draper's shop and the remains of the house above. They abut the Crown Inn, whose chimneys can be seen. The demolition work was carried out by builder Jackie Jackson under the strict(!) health and safety regulations of the time. John Jackson is seen working at top left, with Dougie Parker and John Willie Green also involved.

Above: Captioned 'Storm March 18th 1915 Alston HWA', this traditional Alston winter scene shows snow-blasted buildings in the Potato Market. It was taken by Hugh Walton from near the front of his ironmonger's shop. An excellent photographer who often worked under difficult conditions, he never quite mastered the art of writing backwards on negatives, as the reversed 's' shows.

Whilst Alfred Bales' draper's shop, seen behind the lamp post, was deceptively small, the Crown Hotel, whose partly hidden façade is to the right, was surprisingly large. It extended nearly 130 feet eastwards to a rear courtyard and stables, which were accessed from Crown Lane and the Butts. By the early nineteenth century it was established as one of the district's 'principal coaching inns' and later 'posting houses'. The Crown was famous for its spacious first floor 'long room' or 'Assembly Room' where meetings, dances, Quarter Sessions and even auctions were held. Prior to 1860, the County Court also sat here at bimonthly intervals. Joseph Bland, then for 20 years his widow Ann, were innkeepers from the 1820s to about 1848. After that, the Crown seems to have changed hands regularly until the arrival of Albert V. Dixon *c.*1909. He remained there until at least 1938. The demolition of all the properties on the left-hand side in the early 1960s created a large space, which greatly altered the symmetry of this part of town.

In about 1911/12, some of Alston's old lantern top gas lamps were replaced by a more modern 'swan's neck' style, probably as part of the scheme to commemorate the Coronation of King George V. At the time the one shown here was moved from outside the Temperance Hotel, seen left, to a more visible central position. Behind it is the passageway entrance to Crown Lane, whilst on the extreme right the recently closed Royal Oak Inn, with its sign removed, has not yet become Bales Boarding House.

This postcard was specially produced for Martin Tindle & Son (Henry) of Alston, and whilst its reference number suggests an early 1920s date, the photograph was probably taken several years earlier. There were many quaint, narrow lanes and small squares in the town, but views such as this one are quite scarce because of the difficulties in photographing such confined and poorly lit areas.

Crown Lane, seen here, gave access to the rear of the late eighteenth and early nineteenth century properties lying on the east side of Front Street. Looking uphill towards the Potato Market, the photograph shows Sun Inn Court in the foreground, with the rear entrance to the renamed Sun Temperance Hotel on the right. This was owned and run by Joseph Carr, an ex-coal miner (b.1857) who married Margaret Jane, daughter of innkeeper John Bales (of the Swan and later the Royal Oak). The four-storey building also contained the Union Club and a small shop run by Joseph Henry Henderson, plumber, gasfitter and cycle agent.

The white painted building on the left containing stables, store rooms and a cottage also belonged to the hotel. At its far corner, a branch of Crown Lane led east to the Crown Inn courtyard and stables, before connecting with High Mill Lane and the Butts. When the Sun later became a YHA hostel, the upper floor of the building on the left was converted into a large bunk-room. During the Second World War this housed Italian POWs.

The building on the right beyond the Sun contained the house and shop of Gilbert Graham, general dealer and newsagent. Beyond that lay the old Swan Inn, which had ceased trading by c.1900.

The far outside staircase and veranda gave access to the upstairs offices of Messrs Chater and Atkinson, solicitors, who probably took over John Thompson's practice shortly after 1906. They remained here into the post second war period, later moving to Bank Chambers [Barclays], but leaving their old Front Street sign in place until demolition! For many years they employed the well-known William Thompson as managing clerk. A notable local historian and heavily involved in public life, he died in 1928 aged 74.

Everything seen in this picture was swept away in the post-war 'improvements' of the early 1960s.

Old Alston. 6108

This view of a large group in the upper part of the main Market Place probably dates from c.1905. The Sunday best clothes, song books and conductor with raised arms strongly suggest a religious gathering.

At the time, Mary Kirk had recently retired and closed her drapery and hosiery shop at Pattinson House, behind and to the left of the newly erected gas lamp. The large central four-storey building, dating from the early 1700s, was originally the Sun Inn. Nineteenth century records show that it had many different proprietors, including, during the early 1870s, Blackett Greenwell, the locally noted 'animal preserver' and 'bird stuffer'! After being briefly managed by the photographer Richard Von Dix in 1877, the inn closed down and was bought by Joseph Lancaster (d.1909, aged 60) who operated the adjacent High Mill. Here the three doors with their separate signs indicate its subsequent multipurpose use. For about 30 years the shop and house in the left portion was occupied by 'J. Lancaster, Miller & Bacon Curer'.

The central doorway gave access to the upstairs newsroom, smoking and billiard rooms of the Union Club. This was established in 1889, with Thomas Crawhall-Wilson (Alston House, d.1892) as president, and Joseph Bramwell long-term secretary. The club had about 200 Conservative members in its heyday, but disappears from the records in about 1912.

The right-hand sign, above the door of the small ground floor shop, reads 'J.H. Henderson, Plumber, Gasfitter, Tinsmith & Ironmonger'. Joseph Henry Henderson established his business here in about 1905, having taken over from previous occupant Geo. W. Lee, a watchmaker. Mr Henderson, who was also described as a 'cycle agent and repairer', remained here for about nine years. He then moved to larger premises at the north corner of the Market Place. He later began selling and repairing motor vehicles, eventually building a garage at Townfoot in 1926.

Adjoining to the right was the Ramsay family grocery business. Founded in the 1850s, this had been taken over by Gilbert E. Graham shortly before the photograph was taken.

It seems that Alstonians took every opportunity to gather in large groups and celebrate everything from political and military successes to 'demonstrations' of religious and temperance belief. Such gatherings serve as a poignant reminder of the past importance of faith, the family unit and community, values that were severely eroded by the First World War. Annual gatherings of combined Sunday Schools from the nonconformist churches (Congregational, Primitive and Wesleyan) were often followed by a picnic in nearby fields.

The expansion of day schools in the lead mining districts after 1820 was accompanied by a corresponding growth in Sunday Schools. The London Lead Company, for instance, made attendance at both compulsory for future employment. An 1842 report stated that every place of worship in Alston parish had a school attached. The Sunday School movement was founded nationally in the late eighteenth century, with Alston's first recorded meetings taking place at William Todd's flax mill in about 1800. Todd provided the land on which the new Congregational Chapel was built in 1804, and a Sunday School was officially established at the same time. By 1825 it was attended by 280 children, and a separate school was built opposite the chapel in 1879. Hugh Walton of Alston, who photographed this Whit-Monday scene in 1914, was school superintendent at this chapel and a lifelong supporter of religious education.

By about 1910, the old Sun Inn (closed c.1879), seen in the background, had been re-established by Joseph Carr and family as the Sun Temperance Hotel. It remained in the Carrs' hands until the early 1920s. The signs advertise 'Good Accommodation for Cyclists & Motorists' and 'Post Horses for Hire – moderate charges'.

J.H. Henderson had by this time vacated the small shop at the right-hand side and been replaced, according to the sign above, by 'Holden & Whitfield, Milliners, Fancy Drapers, etc', who only remained there for a short while.

Advert, 1912

A summer market day scene showing the upper part of Market Place c.1900. The empty stalls and handful of customers suggest it is late in the day. Police Sergeant Farrer, on the left, is striding off down Front Street.

Great improvements in the road system in the 1820s meant that a much better supply of food could reach this isolated district from the more fertile farming areas of the Eden Valley, Brampton and Hexham. As a result the thriving Saturday market became increasingly well stocked with a plentiful supply of provisions and other necessities. However, the arrival of the railway in 1852 and growth in local retail outlets slowly eroded its importance. Nonetheless, the Market Place remained a busy area for both business and pleasure on fair days, and also hosted open air meetings and auctions close to the Market Cross.

Alston Co-operative Society was established in 1865 and built its new store, seen centre left, in 1871. At the time membership of the society stood at 150 and the new shop cost about £800. It replaced a small property in the Butts and was described as being 'the most central and prominent shop in the town'. Offering a range of goods including groceries, drapery and footwear, in 1900 there were four staff and 376 members, rising to 463 members and eleven staff by 1905. The society owned five properties in the immediate area by 1914, including the 'Old King's Arms Inn', just visible down Mill Lane in the centre, and still run by Hannah Hetherington (d.1902, aged 82) at the time of this photo. Like her father Anthony Walton, who had operated the business since the 1820s, she was also a wholesale wine and spirit merchant. It closed as an inn c.1901 and was taken over by Joseph Lancaster, a miller and corn merchant from the adjoining High Mill.

To the right is the shop of Miss Mary Kirk ('Draper & Hosier') who retired in about 1903, but continued to live here for many years (d.1923, aged 85). Her parents, George and Margaret, had moved to these premises by 1850. In the 1820s they were recorded as 'linen and woollen drapers'. George Kirk died in 1854, aged 63, and his wife in 1874 aged 76, after which Mary carried on the business. Known as Pattinson House, the building was the birthplace in 1796 of the famous chemist Hugh Lee Pattinson. The Co-op purchased it in 1945 and rebuilt it in 1980. It is now their only shop in Alston.

NOTICE
Is hereby given,
That all nuisances committed in or adjoining to the Alston Market-place by persons improperly depositing Night Soil, Fish Entrails, & other such matters, will be strictly enquired into and presented at the MANOR COURT, and a Fine inflicted by the Jury.

Alston, 13th May, 1859.   **UTRICK BAINBRIDGE**, *Steward.*

PATTINSON, PRINTER, FRONT STREET, ALSTON.

Poster, Alston, 13 May 1859

Alston's famous Market Cross was built in the form of a 'shambles' or covered area where perishable goods, particularly fresh meat, were usually sold. It has had a long and chequered history.

In July 1748, at an earlier unlocated site, John Wesley 'preached at the Cross to quiet staring people who seemed to be little concerned one way or the other'. The present structure was originally erected in 1765 by Sir William Stephenson as a mark of his success and in recognition of his birthplace at Crosslands, Alston. Stephenson was elected Lord Mayor of London in 1764 and knighted shortly afterwards. The Greenwich Hospital, who were then the landowners and Lords of the Manor, requested the replacement of the inscription plaque as it did not acknowledge their permission to build it.

By 1883 the structure was in a dangerous and dilapidated condition and was rebuilt at a cost of £154. Mr H.P. Stephenson, a descendent of Sir William, donated £50 towards the work, with a further £50 provided by the Greenwich Hospital. This was on condition that their ownership of the site was recorded on a new granite plaque (the original 'offending' inscription stone was moved to St Augustine's Church). An ornate iron cross replaced the old gas lantern on the roof, which had incorporated a fixed ladder for the lamplighter.

In 1968 the Market Cross was knocked down by a runaway lorry. It was eventually rebuilt three years later by Kearton & Sons at a cost of £2,000 following extensive enquiries which established the County Council's ownership. The restoration included eight new sandstone support pillars from the Otterburn area, and a small plaque reading 'Re-erected 1970'.

Demolition by a skidding wagon in January 1980 resulted in a further rebuilding by Kearton's at a cost of £4,500, with another inscription, reading 'And 1981', added. At the same time the company replaced the damaged iron cross with a lantern dedicated 'In Memory of Hugh Kearton (1929–1975) a Friend to Alston'.

An elderly resident's vague recollection of a cannon appearing in the Market Place at the end of the First World War is confirmed by this picture, which is thought to show a captured German c.105mm calibre Howitzer. A smaller field gun appeared on the Fair Hill recreation ground at the same time.

Demolished by wagon, January 1980

This c.1925 photograph shows one of the three narrow entrances to the Market Place. It looks north into the Butts, previously a populous part of the town.

The names of Alston's labyrinth of streets and alleyways have changed many times over the last 200 years, but few name plates have ever appeared. This quaint thoroughfare was called Post Office Lane for much of the Victorian era, although the name is now long forgotten. For about 40 years from the mid-1820s until his death in 1866 aged 71, John Dryden served as postmaster at the premises on the left, where he also traded as an ironmonger and newsagent. This was the site of the town's first post office. When his son John took over the business, Phillis Errington became postmistress and the post office moved to her shop on the corner of Edmund's (later Grisdale's) Lane. John Jr. seems to have 'retired' prematurely (aged 35) c.1880, although he continued to live on the premises.

By about 1890, grocers John and Sarah Lee were in business here, succeeded by their son George William, a watchmaker. Around 1914, J.H. Henderson moved into the premises. He was a plumber, ironmonger and cycle dealer, and remained here for about ten years before becoming a garage proprietor. For a short time the shop then became 'The Pharmacy' as seen here. This was run by John Harold Hodgkison, who by 1926 had moved to Bramwell's old shop (next to the Victoria) where he became 'The Chemist'. The property was later purchased by Alston Co-op, serving as their drapery department for many years.

The grocery shop opposite was run by Joseph Seatree (a lead miner) and family from c.1880 to about 1908. It was then bought by the recently widowed Annie Stokoe, whose husband William died in 1906. Mrs Stokoe's shop was a popular place to buy sweets ('bullets'), and she continued in business until the late 1930s (d.1943, aged 81).

On the right is an ancient hostelry, the Turks Head, possibly dating back to 1697. A variant of the Saracen's Head, this traditional name dates back to the Crusades and has an Arabian influence. The arrival of widowed draper Ruth Lee in c.1883 (after a brief period at the Globe) brought stability after a long succession of landlords. She remained here until her death in 1907 aged 68, after which her daughter Elizabeth and husband Hugh (eldest son of Joseph Pattinson of the Angel Inn) took over. They were tenants of Brampton Old Brewery Co. Hugh died in 1939 aged 56, but 'Lillie' continued to run the Turk's Head until 1958. She died the following year aged 83.

Ruth Lee 1839-1907,
Draper & Turk's Head
Innkeeper

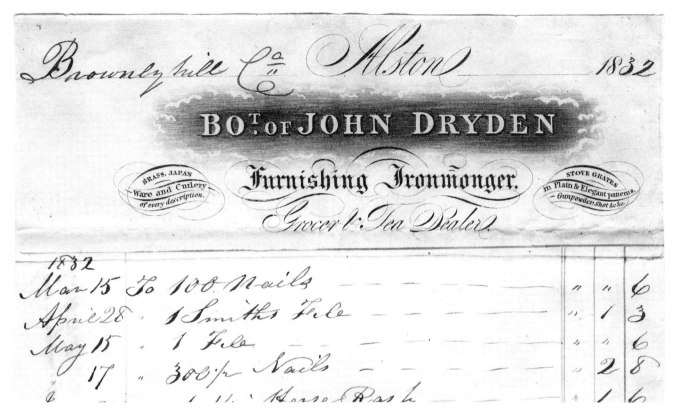

Invoice to Brownley Hill [Mining] Co., 1832

Above: Advert ,1882

Left: Advert ,1924

Right: Bill to Mr J. Walton & Co., Brownley Hill [Mining Co.] for shareholders' meeting (dinner and drinks), 1827

W. ERRINGTON,

TURK'S HEAD, INN,

May 25 Alston 1827

Mr J. Walton & Co. Hill

	£	s.	d.
Breakfast			
Lunch			
Dinner . 25	3	2	6
Fruit			
Tea & Coffee			
Supper			
Ale and Beer	"	10	6
Cyder			
Soda Water			
Port & Sherry	3	12	"
Wine Negus			
Rum and Water			
Brandy and Water . . .	"	16	"
Gin and Water			
Hay & Corn	"	2	6
Paper and Tobacco . . .			
Servants' Eating	8	3	6
Farrier and Smith		2	0
Washing		5	0
Carried over £		13	6

John Pattinson, Printer. Alston

This very rare view looking down the former Post Office Lane dates from the mid- to late 1930s. The lane provided access to many cottages and businesses in the bustling Butts area, including the old Greyhound Inn (centre) with a datestone above the door reading 'WDH 1721'. In 1892 the landlord was Patrick Gilmore, notable mineral dealer and owner of adjoining properties, who was followed by John then Margery McCabe up to the inn's closure c.1902/3.

The unusual detached shop and house on the right was occupied from the 1840s by Joseph and Mary Lee, 'linen & woollen drapers'. Their eldest son Thomas, who married Ruth Spark (b.1839, Garrigill) in 1862, took over the business c.1860. Thomas died in a tragic accident on 5 June 1873 at the nearby 'Skelgill Bottoms' rifle range, east of the town. This was regularly used by the Alston Mountain Rifle Corps and was the venue for the annual New Year 'prize shooting' competition. Three people were involved in the 'ball practice' at the time of the accident. 'Private' Thomas Laidlaw, a shoemaker aged 25, who was briefly managing the Greyhound Inn, had been a Volunteer since 1867. Thomas Lee, aged 45, a recently retired Volunteer corporal and Walton Spark, a 50-year-old gamekeeper were acting as 'markers'. While Laidlaw was firing his second round from 600 yards, Lee stepped out of the target shelter (mantlet) without displaying a danger flag and was hit and killed. The verdict at the following day's inquest was accidental death. His widow Ruth (mother to four children under ten years old) continued to work as a draper until c.1882, briefly managing the Globe Inn before settling at the Turk's Head c.1883.

After being occupied by shoemaker William Holmes, the former drapery shop was purchased in the late 1890s by well-known Garrigill blacksmiths Jonathan (d.1905, aged 82) and his son Thomas Greenwell. Thomas and his wife Margaret, who lived there, originally traded as ironmongers, then became dealers in furniture and household goods, also running a second shop in the Potato Market. 'Tom' died in 1931 aged 68, and 'Maggie' in 1939 aged 75, following a spider bite which became infected.

Rannoch House, on the left, originally a shop, later became home to the Abbot then Beadle families. The Mill Burn (Race) culvert runs from right to left beneath both these properties.

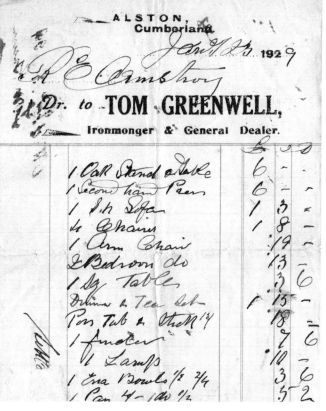

This traffic-free view looking up Front Street is thought to date from c.1930. The Potato Market and H. Walton's prominent ironmonger's shop are visible in the distance. In the centre is one of five trees planted in 1911/12 to commemorate the Coronation of King George V. Their size (and demise) provides a useful means of dating Market Place photos. Several new style swan's neck lamp posts appeared at the same time, one of which is visible in the foreground.

When corn miller Joseph Lancaster died in 1909, the property on the left was bought and reopened as the Sun Temperance Hotel by Joseph Carr (d.1919, aged 60) and his wife Margaret Jane (d.1922, aged 56). By 1923 (as seen here) it was in the hands of Mrs R. Sproat, but within a few years it had become a YHA hostel. The sign over the window of the small annex shop reads 'Lancaster & Co. Bacon Curers, Butchers, Alston Sausages'. It was managed by Geo. Sowerby from Haltwhistle.

The grocery shop adjoining the hotel to the right was opened by Thomas Rutherford in the 1850s. His widow Margaret married miner Thomas Ramsay in 1875, and he carried the business on until his death in 1903, when it was taken over by son-in-law Gilbert E. Graham (a road surfaceman). Later a fruiterer and fish merchant, Gilbert always used a portable sign, seen here propped above the door. His wife Annie Mary ran the business for a few years after his death in 1933, aged 68.

The next property up was part of the old Swan Inn, which closed c.1899. Chater & Atkinson, solicitors, subsequently occupied offices on the upper floors, while prior to 1905 William Salkeld opened a grocery shop on the ground floor. After his death in 1921 (aged 74), this was continued by his wife until about 1930. His parents had a grocery and drapery business near the vicarage (c.1830s–1880s), although young William went to work in London, returning to Alston later.

Further up Front Street, at the top corner of this row, was the old Temperance Hotel. Below this, in the 1930s, Mabel Irving ran a small shop selling home-made pies and sweets, later moving to larger premises opposite. All the buildings described here were demolished in the early 1960s. (How long is the single ladder with 35 rungs?)

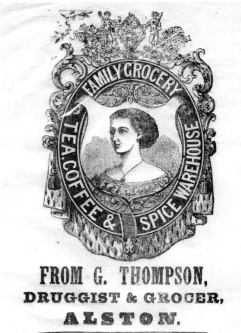

This c.1850s advert was produced by George Thompson, whose business operated from 1814–1891 at the premises seen to the left of the ladder. From 1891 to c.1910 it was run by W. Laws, after which it became J.J. White.

This vibrant market day scene, copied from the original faded and damaged glass negative, shows a fine sunny day in 1899, about 30 years before the previous picture. The buildings look rather drab and unkempt, with the new Alston Rural District Council still to make an impact. Armed with additional powers, it had however succeeded in removing the 'old building' situated where the covered cart stands, although this left unsightly scars on the walls of the Ewe & Lamb (behind the small shelter) and adjoining property. The contentious chemist's shop bay window (now listed, but once described as 'offending') had yet to be built, following in February or March 1900. Seen to the right is 'Laws General Merchant'.

The projecting building with a crowd outside further up the street on the right is the old Black Bull Inn. This was demolished and rebuilt in 1901. The Swan Inn, halfway along the block on the left-hand side, had recently closed down and its sign removed.

Notice in the *Alston Herald* about the introduction of Tuesday half day closing (1874)

This *c*.1912 photo shows a large crowd – possibly a combined Sunday School event – gathered on the west side of the Market Place, with members of the town band grouped to the left. In other photographs the minister (bottom right) can be seen standing on a soap box. At the upper left is the Ewe & Lamb Inn, which first appears in records in the 1840s. When the photograph was taken it was owned by Mrs Mary Gill. Before that it had been run for about 35 years from the mid-1860s by ex-ironstone miner William Greenwell and his wife Isabella. The shop to the right was established in 1814 as a 'druggist and grocer' by John Thompson. His son George (b.1820, Alston) continued the business for over 50 years until his death in 1891, when it was transferred to William Laws. By 1910 it had passed – as the sign shows – to John J. White, a 'general merchant' who remained there until the later 1930s, after which R. Wright & Sons, 'fruiterers and florists', took over. The old Globe Inn next door had about ten landlords between 1820 and its closure in the later 1880s, being run as a temperance hotel by Sarah Harrison in its final few years. It is seen here having been converted to a house and shops, with the central passageway leading to Globe Lane and two cottages to the rear. John Thomas Walton ('Boot Maker and Dealer' seen on sign) was born in Kates Lane, Alston, in 1861. He married at Nenthead in 1883 and worked there until 1886 when he returned to Alston to rejoin his father William. William, from Renwick (born *c*.1831), had begun the family business in the 1850s. John bought this property in about 1901, moving the shop from across the Market Place, with the family living upstairs. After his early death in 1903 (aged 43), his son Joseph William continued as a 'Boot & Clog Maker' until his retirement in 1950. He died in 1962, aged 78.

The shop next door, described as a 'Cycle Depot', was set up *c*.1910 by James William Kirsopp (b.1877 Leadgate; d.1962) who, with his wife Sarah, also ran the post office and grocery store at Garrigill from about 1905. He remained here for several years before moving next door (right) into the old premises of Adamson Pickering, butcher (formerly J.J. Shield; d.1910, aged 61) where he also sold and repaired motorcycles. He was later joined by his son Charles William ('Willie', b.1911, Garrigill), who continued the business into the 1970s. During the 1920s and 30s, their old shop (seen here) was occupied by Joseph Lowe, a gents tailor.

Advert from touring map, *c*.1920s

The Market Place, originally part of Raise Tenement, had three very narrow street entrances which in ancient times could be sealed off to form a defensible area. This enigmatic photograph shows the irregularly shaped old building (a house, shop and workshop) which adjoined the top entrance, obscuring an open view of the town centre. The building is symbolic of a time of change and the start of a new era. Alston Rural District Council (RDC) first met on 28 December 1894, and in November 1898 applied for additional 'Urban Powers' under the Health Acts of 1875 and 1890. These dealt with a range of issues including water supplies, the disposal of waste and sewage, and the purchase and condemning of dangerous and uninhabitable properties. In 1898, to improve access to the Market Place, protracted negotiations began to acquire the 'old building' in order to demolish it and open out Front Street – here only 9 feet wide. Mr J. Roberts, who also owned the house and small shop on the left (on to which he proposed to later add a bay window) was offered £350 for the property. At the same time, the Greenwich Hospital were approached and agreed (indenture dated April 1900) to sell their 999 year ground leases, dating from 1611 and 1621.

It seems likely that this posed photograph of c.1899 shows members of the council sub-committee that was set up to progress the matter. Despite this, it eventually resulted in an unsatisfactory outcome in court in 1901. Their suggested identities (from left to right down the stairs, with ages) are: Albert Walton (25) shoemaker with workshop here (later moved to Hexham); Henry Walton (77) of Howburn, RDC Chairman and JP (d.1908); 'Major' Thomas W. Dickinson (50) of Tower Hill, RDC Clerk (d.1901); John Millican (77, wearing top hat) of Croft House, RDC Vice Chairman and JP (d.1901); George W. Storey (44, to left) of South Tyne House, RDC (later Chairman) and JP (d.1940); Joseph R. Walton? (44, papers and rule in hand) of Lowbyer Manor House, RDC, JP, a land and estate agent. The photographer was Thomas Bramwell (64), also a member of the RDC and JP (d.1907).

Between 1895 and 1902 this area was the subject of lengthy negotiations. These initially centred on its repair and improvement by the Greenwich Hospital, but later concerned the transfer of the Market Place to the RDC. These failed when it transpired the Council had no legal powers to operate a market, which involved 'tolls and remuneration of toll collector'. Many years later, in 1944/45, both market areas were sold to Cumberland County Council for £7.

By late 1899, negotiations between Mr Roberts, the RDC and others had resulted in the demolition of the 'old building' and alteration of the adjoining property, seen on the left in the previous picture. The attachment of the 'out of character' curved glass, sloping-fronted bay window was the subject of considerable controversy. It was built following several site visits, a number of reports, plus requests to define boundaries and various solicitors' submissions. Initially the RDC refused permission twice, eventually accepting an amended plan in February 1900.

An outcry followed. The Parish Council 'declared itself in deadly opposition to the encroachment upon the public footpath', demanding 'that nothing else than its entire removal will satisfy it'. The flustered RDC recanted, taking legal action. However, at the June 1901 County Court case, the defendant was found 'not guilty' and the window (now listed) remained in situ. Owner Joseph Roberts (b.1853, Stoke on Trent), chemist and druggist of Stella House, Blaydon, also fitted an etched glass window showing a pestle and mortar and 'J.R. AD 1900' into the old first floor doorway (seen centre). The narrow Kates Lane archway is to the left.

Roberts also operated a larger shop at Church Street, Blaydon (bought c.1895 from Mr Miller, a specialist in bottled 'mixture cures') and his son Joseph Asquith Roberts, also a chemist, ran the Alston & District Drug Co. store until the early 1920s, when he returned to Blaydon (d.1938, aged 57). If the figure seen here is Joseph Asquith (b.1881, Newcastle), which seems likely, his age (c.30–35) would date

the photograph to between 1911 and 1916. Adverts in the window promote products including Robert's foot rot paste, Virol, bile beans and pile pills.

By 1924 Joseph Roberts had been succeeded by James Adair Clues (b.1899, Gateshead), an optician, who continued the business under the same name until his death in 1957, aged 58. As well as selling spectacles, remedies, toilet preparations and presents, he offered a wide range of photographic services and materials, including his own series of postcards. He was a Freemason, a JP, chorister, churchwarden and secretary of St Augustine's – about which he compiled an authoritative historical record. He lived in Croft Terrace and during the Second World War was chief air raid warden and captain in the Home Guard, as well as a founder member of Alston British Legion.

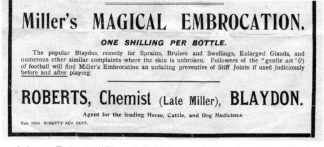

Advert, Roberts (Chemist) Alston and Blaydon, Dec. 1904

At this point Front Street changes direction, opening out into the natural centre of the town, with its picturesque cobbled market area. The surrounding buildings, made of sandstone with flagged roofs, several with outside stairs, were well established in this pattern by the time the first map of Alston was drawn up in 1775. Permission to build the tenement style properties facing the camera, 'adjoining upon the churchyard wall', with shops either side of a central doorway and accommodation above, was given by the Lord of the Manor in 1697. Others were added a few years later. The dimensions of the original sites, measuring about 10 yards wide by 5 yards deep, are little changed today.

This Valentine Series postcard has special appeal because it was updated several times by the addition of suitably dressed figures, to cover a sale period of about 25 years. The left-side window display, old style lamp post and lack of trees indicate the original photograph was taken c.1906–10. Working from the left, businesses around the Market Place at that time were: chemist J.A. Roberts; Ewe & Lamb Inn (Rob. Earnshaw, living upstairs [l.u.]); boot and shoemaker Jos. W. Walton, l.u.; butcher John J. Shield, l.u.; newsagent and stationer with lending library John G. Lee, l.u.; hairdresser James Nicholson, l.u.; London, City & Midland Bank.

Partly seen at the bottom, from the left, are: grocer John Pickering, l.u. and Sarah Pattinson, l.u., confectioner with 'refreshment rooms'; draper and milliner Mary Welsh, l.u. and boot and clog maker John G. Scholick, l.u., at white-sheeted window. The latter building had four storeys at the time, but was later converted to three. Next along is grocer and furniture dealer John G. Cranston, l.u.; draper and milliner Sarah J. Kearton (with light shop awning), l.u. with husband Hugh, builder and joiner. She died in 1912, after which the business was taken over by Margaret Bramwell. After that is butcher Thomas Spark, earlier l.u., later Nentholme House. Finally, at extreme right, just out of view, stood the shop of grocer John Lee, l.u., succeeded by his son, watchmaker

George W. Lee, l.u. The shelter in the foreground stands on the site (purchased by the RDC in 1902 for £12/10s) of the original six-pillared market shambles. This appears on the 1775 map and is recorded as early as 1741.

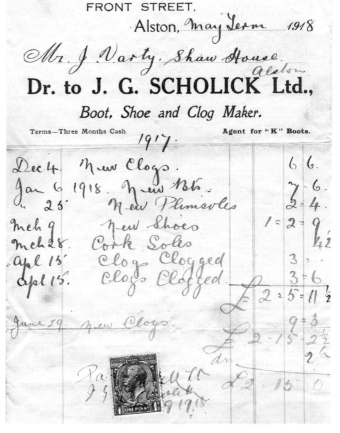

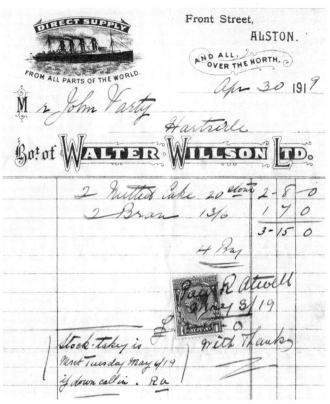

Invoice to John Varty, farmer, Hartside, 1919. W. Willson Ltd leased these premises in 1912, buying the property from Sarah Hall in 1926 for £800.

NEW SADDLERY AND HARNESS MAKING ESTABLISHMENT.

HARRISON HALL

RESPECTFULLY informs the Public of Alston and surrounding district that he has commenced the above business in a Shop near the Wesleyan Chapel, ALSTON, and, having secured a good Workman, he trusts that by attention to the requirements of his customers he will merit and secure a liberal share of public patronage.

Advert, *Alston Herald*, May 1874

Harrison Hall's shop and house, with basement below, stood on a sloping site in Front Street above the entrance to Kates Lane, adjoining the premises of J. Roberts, chemist. The formal shop fronts and regular line of Front Street contrasted starkly with the rather haphazard alleyway and courtyard developments of much of the rest of the town. Old photos show a striking similarity in style between several of the frontages here. Many probably date from the mid-nineteenth century, the peak period of Alston's business expansion when its population was greatest, prior to the collapse of lead mining. Most shops had fluted timber columns with decorated heads, a consoled canopy overhang, arched-top window sections and similar doors and fanlights. The adjoining doors usually led to living accommodation above.

Harrison Hall (born *c*.1855, Alston) set up in business as a saddler near St Paul's Wesleyan Chapel in 1874, although his father and elder brother were coal merchants. He lived at Townhead with his mother until 1894, when he married Sarah Falder (b.1867, Gamblesby) – probably around the time he bought these premises in Front Street. He also later owned two warehouses and two cottages behind in Kates Lane.

Seen here on the steps of his shop *c*.1905, Harrison Hall continued to trade as a saddler, ironmonger and furniture dealer, with a game licence (granted by the RDC in July 1895) until 1912. After that, Walter Willson (grocers) leased the property, trading here until 1977. Harrison moved to a small shop on Station Road, below Spring House, remaining there until his death in 1923, aged 69. His daughter Sally continued in business into the 1930s as an ironmonger, also selling 'fishing tackle, ammunition and sports accessories'.

In spite of heavy horse traffic there were usually only two or three saddlers and harness makers in the district. John W. Atkinson (Front Street) operated from the 1840s, transferring the business to Joseph Craig *c*.1874, who continued it until the early 1880s. At this time William Collinson from Penrith (b.1839) set up business in the Potato Market, later moving to Front Street (near the Quaker Meeting House) and finally to King's Arms Lane (near the Masonic Hall). He retired *c*.1912 and died in 1917, aged 78. John Smith (Townhead) went into business *c*.1905 to be succeeded by John Thompson between 1914 and 1920.

Kate's Lane Alston. H.W

A 1920s writer was captivated by Alston's 'narrow, twisted, stony, quaint, irregular lanes, alleys and closes'. In the 1930s, another visitor was taken with its toppling blocks of buildings, divided not by streets, but endless passages paved with cobbles, leading from one courtyard to another and stone stairways everywhere. However, despite the town's picturesque appearance, the second author noted that 'the local sanitary authorities have a baleful eye turned on its quaint jumble'. He added that instead of 'devastating the beauty and quaintness of the place (which is an asset of growing importance) they might take those extra pains to preserve it'. Alston, he stated, 'is a proper case for those societies and trusts which make a boast of preserving the rural amenities'.

Whilst, as he feared, much has been lost in the last 70 years, a surprising amount has survived – albeit modified in some form. This scarce c.1910 view by Hugh Walton shows Kates Lane, part of which still remains intact, doubtless protected by its 'hidden' aspect and 'impossible' access. The lane, which appears to have had no other name, originally led to Kates Bottom, part of a field attached to Temple Croft House. The lower buildings and courtyard in the photograph formed the Maltings (locally 'Mautin') which included the old malt-house, later converted to cottages. Plans to demolish and redevelop this area under Slum

Clearance Acts were put forward in 1956. A left turn from the Maltings led past Garden House and cottages into the Mustard Field (with barns), leased by H. Hall.

Residents in this early artisan area increased in number from 94 in 1841 (when there were twenty occupied properties and six empty ones) to a peak of 131 in 1851 (twenty-nine properties, none vacant). At this time there were thirteen boot and shoemakers and three tailors in the area. By 1881 numbers had declined to 67 (fourteen occupied properties and thirteen empty), falling further to only 34 people in 1891 (nine occupied buildings; seventeen empty). The rapid reduction followed the collapse of lead mining and subsequent migration from the town.

By 1910 there had been a small increase, with thirteen cottages occupied, six of them owned by William Little, wine and spirit merchant. The change in fortunes was temporary, however, and in c.1920 the area was described as 'three parts empty' but 'paradise for an artist'. The cottage on the left was owned by Thomas Davidson (51, coal miner) in c.1910, and the two beyond (sharing joint stairs) by H. Hall, saddler. His tenants were Francis Lee (first door) and widow Mary Robson (52, charwoman) standing at the second one. In July 1932, workmen found a stone piscina (font) in the Maltings below. Marked '1721-ICI', this was later presented to the church.

This rare *c*.1900 photograph shows High Mill Lane looking down towards the Butts. The towering corn mill ('Lancaster's') at upper left occupied an advantageous position very close to the Market Place. Originally owned by Greenwich Hospital Estates, it was completely rebuilt in 1767–9 at a cost of £250. The work was carried out by their Receiver, the famous civil engineer John Smeaton FRS, with a stable and miller's living quarters added shortly afterwards (cost £54). The mill contained machinery for shelling, drying and grinding corn with three sets of stones. Its 'pitch back' wheel was of unusual design, measuring 30 feet in diameter but only 10 inches wide, and featuring a unique 'scooped' water feed. During extensive alterations and repairs in 1817, the overhead wooden mill race leats were replaced with cast-iron underground pipes and a new 21 foot, 26 inch wide 60 bucket wheel fitted. The mill was leased for periods of 21 years, in 1800 being let to William Todd who was replaced shortly afterwards by William Greenwell. He was followed by Hetherington & Peart, then Robert Nattrass (1842), while from 1863 until *c*.1930 the Lancaster family operated it.

The ground floors of the building seen in the centre (with the cart outside) were used as a slaughterhouse and storeroom by Thomas Spark, the butcher at Cross House shop. He was succeeded by Matt. Jackson during the 1920s. In the 1930s the storeroom at the east end of the premises was converted to a fish and chip shop by Lance Jackson. The Armstrongs, and later the Ramsays, lived upstairs, and the building was demolished in the 1960s. The detached house and shop glimpsed in the background belonged to Thomas and Margaret Greenwell. It was demolished in the 1950s.

Whilst some families lived upstairs in the properties on the right, the ground floors were for commercial use. At the bottom end were stables and warehouses (bearing the date stone 'IWA 1750') owned by the Co-op. Part of it was later used as a slaughterhouse, again by Cross House butchers, first Tom Burns and later Sydney Blackstock, who moved to the Nentsberry abattoir at the start of the second war. Further up was a joinery shop and sawmill belonging to builder Robert W. Snowdon of Townhead. This whole block (rebuilt by Keartons 1961/62) was taken over during the Second World War by North East Coast Aircraft Components Ltd. (NECACO) and became known as the 'Top Factory'. In the post-war period Precision Products set up in business here and at the adjoining High Mill, which they bought in 1947. They specialised in high quality castings using the new 'Shaw Process'.

Advert, *Carlisle Journal*, 25 September 1863

HIGH MILL,

Alston, 185

Mr Jacob Walton

Bot. of ROBERT NATTRASS,

DEALER IN

Flour, Rye, Oatmeal, Peas, Barley, &c.

1852					
May 22d	1	bag	bran	4/.	4
Oct 1st	2	do	do	3/6	7
Dec 14	1	do	do		3 6
1853 Jany 4	1	do	do		3 6
25	2	do	do		7
–	2	pks	Barley	3/6	7
					£1.12

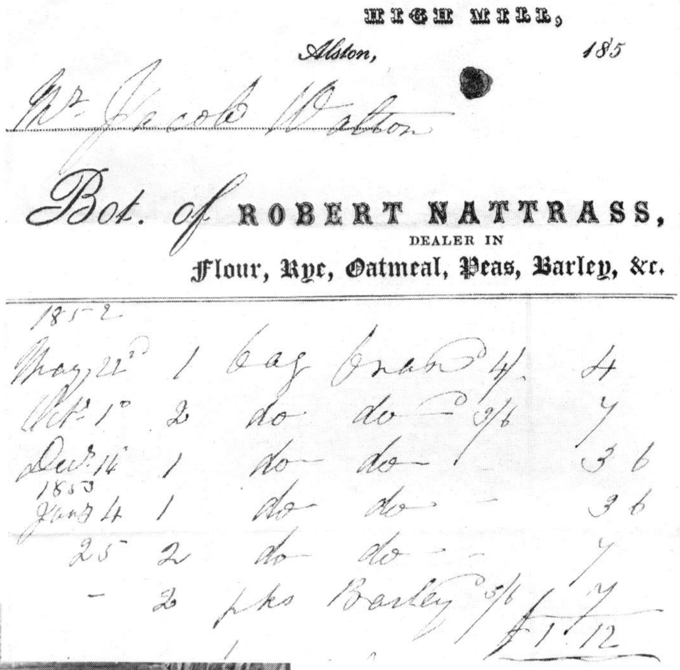

High Mill invoice to Jacob Walton (Greenends), 1852

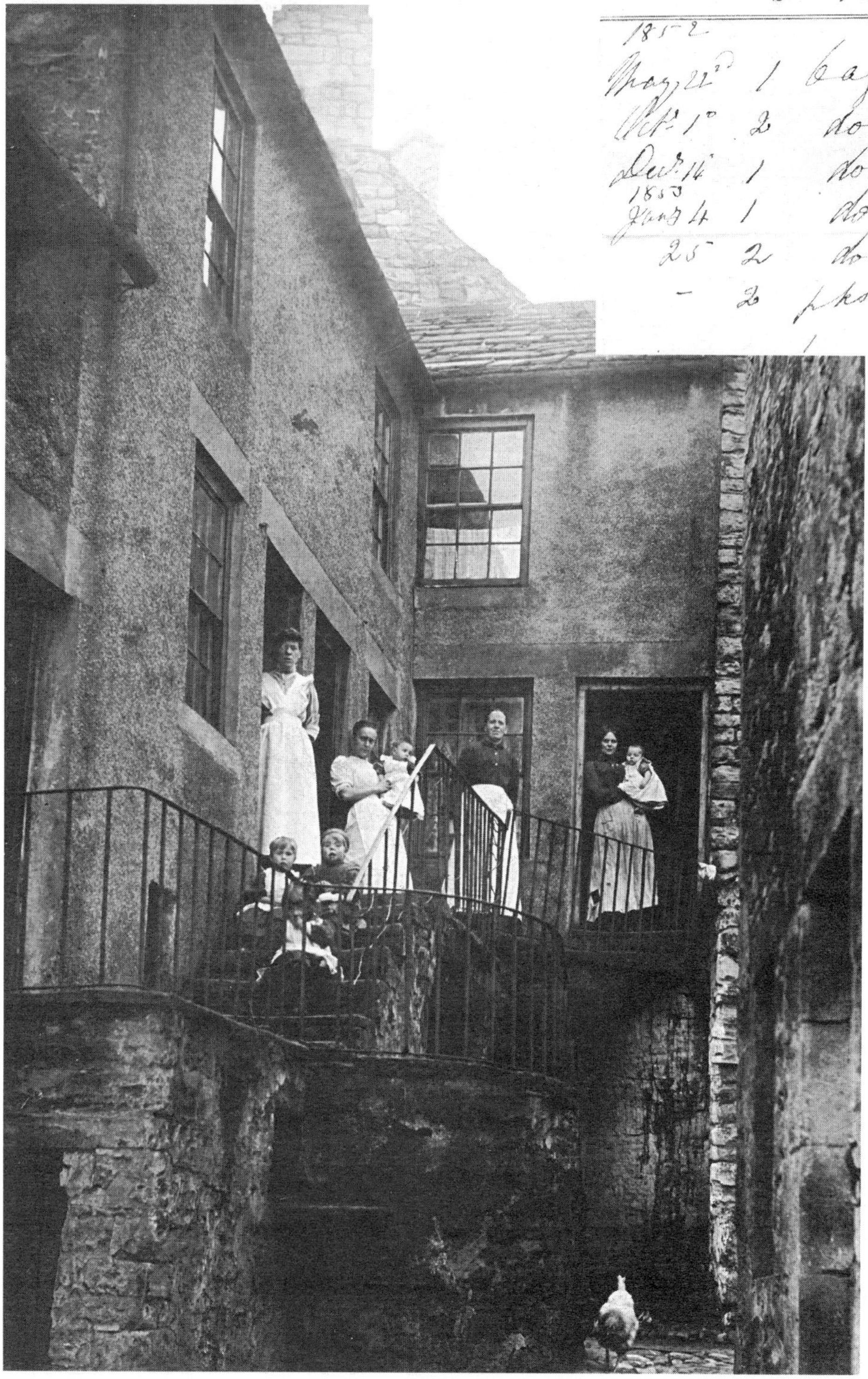

Entitled 'A Bit of Alston HWA', this scarce Edwardian postcard view was taken by Hugh Walton, again seen testing his photographic techniques in dark and dingy places. The obscure setting is the junction of Old Kings Arm's Lane and High Mill Lane, located at the south corner of the large corn mill (its east wall is seen on the right, looking SSW). The cottages, with railed landings to upper floors, survive in disguised form to this day. Having been converted into a 'transformer station' by the Yorkshire Electric Power Co. in 1942, they escaped the demolition that later befell neighbouring properties. The transformer station was probably to serve the adjoining, then new, Top Factory. Alston's 11,000 volt mains electric supply line from Penrith over Hartside was not completed until October 1934. Previously the cottages' occupants had included families of Ramsays and Thompsons, and later Herdmans. If the little boy on the top step is Percy Beadle (a Ramsay relative, b. July 1902) the photograph was taken *c.*1904.

An early Edwardian photograph of Hugh Kearton's joinery shop, located in the commercial section of the upper Butts area, in what was previously Post Office Lane. Owner Hugh (seen right) and his twin brother Thomas were born into a farming family at Rotherhope, near Alston, in 1853. Hugh trained as a joiner, later working for noted Weardale architect and builder George Race, who specialised in the design and construction of Wesleyan chapels. After completion of Haltwhistle Chapel in 1878, Hugh set up his own business at Townhead, Alston. One of his first projects was to assist with the rebuilding of the fire-damaged woollen mill. In 1883 he married Sarah Jane Milburn, whose parents owned a grocery and drapery business in the Market Place. Sarah, a milliner, later took over the family shop and the couple lived in the apartment above for many years. They brought up three sons there, Hugh, Tom and Fred. In 1891, for a short period, Hugh moved his business from Townhead to the sawmill premises at 'New Road' on the corner of Thirlwalls (King's Arms) Lane. These had been vacated by the deceased Thomas Richardson, joiner and millwright (d.1888?, aged 64). Later on, Hugh Kearton acquired the joinery shop seen here.

He greatly expanded the Kearton building company, which retained these old workshops until the 1960s, in later years making coffins here for its long established undertaker's business. H. Kearton & Sons, which continued operating into the 1990s, later took over larger premises further down the lane which were used as workshops and stores. For a time after the First World War the company also had a sawmill adjoining the gasworks.

Hugh, seen here in typical pose with bowler hat and saw, surrounded by sections of sliding-sash windows, died in May 1923, aged 70. He had been a widower for twelve years. The wall on the right (with a horse-sledge leaning against it) was part of the original building used by the Co-operative Society as a warehouse and stables. It later provided garaging for the society's small delivery van, the first of which was acquired in the mid-1930s. The property was badly damaged by fire in 1959, with the narrow lanes hindering fire engine access. Adjoining on the left but out of view was the Greyhound Inn. This was latterly run by widow Margery McCabe and closed about the time the photograph was taken, after which it was converted to a house.

NOTICE OF REMOVAL

MR. HUGH KEARTON

BEGS TO INTIMATE TO THE PUBLIC OF

ALSTON,

And neighbourhood, that he has now Removed from Town Head to the

SHOP & SAW-MILL

LATELY OCCUPIED BY

MR. T. RICHARDSON,

Where he intends carrying on, in addition to his other business,

All the branches of Saw-mill work.

He also takes this opportunity of returning thanks for all favours received during the past, and trusts, that by strict and prompt attention he may secure a continuance of them in the future.

Alston, July 7th, 1891.

W. Pattinson, Printer, Market Square, Alston.

The Butts is a gently sloping area of land that curves around the north-east side of the churchyard. It closely follows the course of the Mill Burn (Race), from High Mill down towards King's Arms Lane. As its name implies, it was originally open ground used for archery practice, which was compulsory for all males aged between sixteen and sixty as late as the reign of Henry VIII. The Alston 'Paine [fine] Roll' of 1597 states 'That the Butts of Alston and Garrigill be yearly made before Snt. Hellens Day [3 May] upon Payne of 3s.4d for every default'.

Compared with the relative formality of Front Street, the Butts was a quaint but disorganised development, much of it built in the eighteenth century. The first reference in manorial records appears in 1750, and describes 'drayns … frome the several houses newly erected in the Butts'. Built of stone, many of the properties reflected the old Border defensive style, with byres on the ground floor and living quarters above, accessed by external stairs. Soon after 1900, the new Rural District Council (formed in 1894) began to condemn such houses. Many sets of outside stairs were removed and accommodation extended to the ground floors. The building on the extreme left of the photograph (featuring a door lintel inscribed 'TIB 1752' [Thomas Bateman]) has been altered in this way.

In about 1850, when lead mining and the local population peaked, some 400 residents – including many tradespeople – lived in the Butts. However, by 1900 this number had shrunk to c.150. When the photograph was taken around the time of the First World War, these properties in the Low Butts were occupied by Walton Saunders (up the steps to the left), Mary Thompson (centre) and Francis Pickering (the door on the right). Later, following demolition, the site formed part of Kearton & Sons builder's yard. Opposite here across the lane lies Green Square and Garden House, from the later 1930s occupied by butcher George A. Honeyman. Behind the square are the Salvin Schools, both of which were designed by D. Rome and named after their principal benefactor, the Revd Hugh Salvin RN (at Alston from 1841 until his death in 1852, aged 79). The Girls' School opened in 1844 and the Infants' in 1851. To the left of the three figures is a courtyard called Sunset View which contained several cottages, stables and a slaughterhouse. At the time these were all owned by butcher Thomas Spark, who lived in adjoining Nentholme House.

Beyond the figures, up the lane on the left-hand side, was a blacksmith's shop that was operated for nearly thirty years by Harrop Holmes, who died in 1928 aged 71. This property and the warehouse and cottage adjoining (which bears the datestone 'MWE 1739' and was later called Rasper House) were owned by his step-brother Tom Greenwell. Both were initially Garrigill blacksmiths.

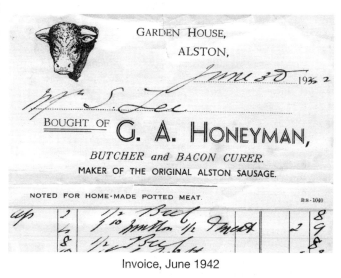

Invoice, June 1942

At least three churches are known to have stood on this prominent site close to the town centre. This very unusual photograph was taken by Thomas Bramwell c.1885 and shows the third and present structure without a spire.

In the twelfth century King Henry II (1154–89) appointed his clerk Galfrid as Rector of Alston, the benefice later (1378) coming under the control of Hexham Priory. Archdeacon Sharp ordered repairs to the decaying first church in 1723, and by 1763 a successor had recommended rebuilding it completely 'as the present fabrick is so ruinous in every part that it can never be effectively repaired'. Possibly incorporating twelfth century sections, the original church, dedicated to St Augustine, first Archbishop of Canterbury, measured 67 by 35 feet and comprised a chancel, nave and north aisle.

The Revd Thomas Lancaster (d. 1789), who was appointed as vicar in 1756, raised £754 from around 320 local and London supporters towards building the second church. Benefactors included Greenwich Hospital, the London Lead Co. and former 'natives of Alston'. Plans were drawn up by John Smeaton, with designs and costings by Carlisle architect John Nicholson. The church was built in stone with a Cumberland slate roof by Messrs. Stephenson and Smith in 1769 . It measured 66 feet long by 40 feet wide 'without a pillar', and included a nave, two aisles, chancel ('far too small'), a 12 foot square tower and a gallery. The interior was completed in spring 1770, the final cost reaching £1,062.

In 1769, a report to the Bishop of Durham described 'the inhabitants [of Alston] much at variance and some very clamorous'. This referred to disputed allocations of pew and gallery seating, with 200 'free sittings' and the rest assigned. The dispute was finally settled in June 1771 by four paid Commissioners who let 75 pews for c.£60 p.a. By this stage the total cost of the church had risen to £1,134/0/10d.

Originally described as 'a large handsome building, tolerably well executed', pride in the new church subsequently dwindled. Although referred to as 'a good church of modern structure' (1811) and 'neat and well-built' (1840), by 1858 it was falling out of favour and had become 'a plain stone building'. It was eventually labelled 'destitute of architectural features and without ornamentation of any kind'.

The reasons for its replacement after only 100 years are not recorded, but may have included its size, plain design, poor condition or the recent completion (1868) of a 'dominant' new Wesleyan Chapel (St Paul's). These factors are likely to have been combined with a desire for contemporary Victorian splendour. Having been demolished under a licence dated April 1869 at a cost of £74/11/-, it was replaced by the fine, though rather incongruous, new building seen above.

Second church (1770), photographed by Von Dix (c.1868)

This elevated view, probably by Thomas Bramwell, was taken from the Town Hall clock tower in 1886 and shows the new (third) St Augustine's Church. Built on the site of its predecessor in Early English style, it was designed by architect John Wilson Walton of London. The building consisted of a chancel, nave, south aisle and tower with 'free' seating for about 450. C.&J.S. Armstrong, builders of Carlisle, erected it for a 'basic' cost (no spire) of £4,245/15/8d. Details of the rebuilding were placed beneath the foundation stone at the buttress of the chancel arch. These included the names of the fourteen 'worthies', chaired by the Revd W.C.P. Baylee (vicar from 1862 until his death in 1873) who had raised £3,800 to commence work. The stone itself was laid on 18 August 1869 by Mrs Wilson of Shotley Hall, whose husband Thomas pledged ten per cent of the building costs.

When the church opened on 30 August 1870 it 'was in a very unfinished state'. Dr Baring, Lord Bishop of Durham, presided at the opening, but had objected to a figure of St Augustine being placed in the niche above the main entrance, as it would have put him above the carving of Christ. The niche is still empty today. Many gifts and donations followed, including £250 for the east window from Mrs Salvin, in memory of her husband Hugh (vicar from 1841–52). In 1874, £207 was paid for carving capitals, corbels and other ornaments, while in 1878 Bryceson Bros. & Ellis of London fitted a new organ, 'built on a grand scale', at a cost of £670.

A 55 foot tower with 60 foot spire was originally planned in 1869, but only 30 feet of the buttressed tower was initially erected. It was completed in 1886, along with the spire, at a cost of £1,170, of which Miss Hodgson (Salkeld Hall, Penrith) paid £700; the architect was G.D. Oliver of Carlisle.

The tower lacks the strength to allow the present peal of ten bells to be rung conventionally. Instead, they are struck by their clappers with ropes attached to a small keyboard or carillon. Six of the bells were installed in 1949 in memory of Henry and Jessie Walton. They include the famous 1714 Derwentwater Bell, presented by Greenwich Hospital in 1767 (recast 1845 by Rob. Watson, Newcastle and again in 1949 by Gillett & Johnston, Croydon). The other four date from 1950 and commemorate Midland Bank manager and churchwarden A.G.S. Steele who was murdered on 13 September 1949.

The church's beautiful reredos was donated in 1900 by Miss Horrocks, and the large oak First World War memorial screen was erected in 1920. The three Front Street buildings seen in the foreground of the photograph are all inns – the King's Arms, adjoining Thirlwalls Lane (left), with the Angel in the centre and Church Gates near the steps.

Left: This Thomas Bramwell photograph of c.1887 shows the Church Gates area looking east. The main entrance to St Augustine's Church is under the arch, while a second narrow passageway, about 50 yards to the right, provided access from the Market Place. The old iron gate under the arch was made in 1769 by Jacob Smith for £1/9/-. In 1887/8, the archway and the three houses to its right were demolished. A new gateway, including wall, railings and pillars with lanterns was constructed in their place. The work cost £420, and was designed to improve access and allow an open view of the church from Front Street.

During the period that Revd E.L. Bowman was vicar (1875–89), about £2,500 was raised for this and other improvements. Replacement oak gates were made by Kearton & Sons in 1938, at a cost of £28/10/0. They were paid for by the Greenwich Hospital and feature two carved panels (by Fred Kearton) which symbolise church and parish history. One shows the Cross of St Cuthbert, and serves as a reminder of the unusual position of Alston as an ancient parish of Northumberland with its place in the Diocese of Durham until 1882. It then became part of the newly created Diocese of Newcastle, stretching from Tyne to Tweed. The other panel shows the arms of the Greenwich Hospital for Seamen. In 1735 the Hospital was granted the Derwentwater Estates (including much of Alston Moor), which were forfeited to the Crown after James, the 3rd Earl, was beheaded for his part in the 1715 Jacobite Rebellion. For over 200 years Greenwich Hospital supported the church, and from 1812 held full patronage and the right to appoint the vicar. Between 1835 and 1926, nine of the thirteen incumbents were naval chaplains. In 1952 the patronage was handed to the Bishop of Newcastle.

The cottage to the left of the arch, bordering the churchyard, was retained following reconstruction of the entrance. Its stairs were rebuilt within an enclosed, galleried porch which survives to this day. After 1900, the building, which abuts the Church Gates Inn, was used as offices by Blackburn & Main, solicitors.

Middle and bottom: When Dilston Hall near Corbridge, the home of James Radcliffe, 3rd Earl of Derwentwater (beheaded in 1716) was being demolished, John Smeaton, 'Receiver' (managing agent) for owners Greenwich Hospital Estates, arranged for the bell and this clock to be presented to 'Aldstone Church'. The church was about to be rebuilt and the donation was approved in a Commissioners Board minute dated 28 August 1767. The early seventeenth century single pointer clock was dismantled and despatched in April 1770. Isaac Hall was paid 13/8d to carry the clock and T. Sowerby 2/6d to transport the face.

The clock was never installed and lay neglected for 200 years. In 1977 parishioners and friends raised £974 (in memory of 47 departed, named on a plaque) for it to be restored by Will. Potts & Sons, clockmakers of Leeds. With local help, it was finally installed in St Augustine's Church 'as a working exhibit'. A new glass fibre face was donated by David Dowding; stone weights in leather slings were provided by Tim Meagher; and joinery work was undertaken by Kearton & Sons. The restored clock is barely recognisable from its appearance in this undated old photograph.

This unusual photograph, probably taken by T. Bramwell *c.*1887, looks west towards the original church gateway, seen in the centre. The three properties on the left formed the 'bottom narrows' of Front Street and were demolished soon after, along with the adjoining archway extensions. The new pathway followed a straight course from the gas lamp to the main street, greatly improving the view of the church.

Alston churchyard interments ceased 'By Order' on 1 June 1860, the last funeral taking place on 21 May. Closure followed new legislation regarding burial grounds close to habitation, drawn up 'for the protection of public health'.

Mary Brown (73) of Thirlwalls (King's Arms) Lane was the first person to be buried in the 'New Cemetery'. Her funeral took place on 24 June 1860. The site at the Firs, initially covering about 2 acres, was later extended to 3.3 acres. It was consecrated by the Bishop of Durham on 2 April 1862, when '... a Commodious Tent was erected for the occasion'.

The churchyard seen here contains many interesting gravestones, including several decorated medieval ones and others dating from the late seventeenth and early eighteenth century. One of these commemorates James Kirton, 'the ingenious clockmaker', who was buried in 1729. Another is the anonymous 'Cobbler's Stone' (possibly James Jefferson, d.1783), complete with poetic epitaph. In the immediate foreground is the grave of the author's namesake(!), [Revd] Peter Wilkinson, who died in December 1858, aged 67.

ALSTON NEW CEMETERY.—The Home Office having prohibited the use of the Old Church Yard, for the purpose of interring the dead, the Burial Board have laid out a fine and level piece of ground, about two acres in extent, as a cemetery, a short distance to the south of the town. The 31st ultimo was the last day allowed by the order, interments will therefore take place in the New Cemetery forthwith.

Carlisle Patriot, 9 June 1860

Above: advert 1888. *Below:* advert 1894

This *c.*1870 photograph of the seventeenth century Angel Inn was taken by Richard Von Dix (b.1834, Llanrhidian, Swansea) using the messy wet collodion process. As its name implies, the inn lies close to the church. One of three adjoining taverns seen on page 60, refurbishment work prior to 1886 saw the installation of larger bay windows and the removal of its door hood. By 1910 the building included an attic dormer.

The Angel Inn was mainly run by widowed members of the Pattinson family for at least 135 years up to 1925. Early records show Sarah (d.1842, aged 75) being succeeded by son Hugh, a joiner (d.1857, aged 58) and his wife Mary Ann (I). Assisted by her daughter Elizabeth ('Betsy'), she remained in charge until her death in 1889, aged 85. Elizabeth (b.1846; d.1937, aged 91) acceded to the estate which comprised the inn, a nearby house, cottages, stables and barns. In 1893 she married 'Major' Thos. W. Dickinson of Lovelady Shield (and later Tower Hill), letting the business to her nephew Joseph, a joiner (d.1897, aged 47) and his wife Mary Ann (II). Widowed with seven children, she remained as landlady until her death in 1925, aged 69, when Jn. Wright took over.

Out of view to the right is the Church Gates Inn, which features mullioned windows, a fire window, door hood and a lintel inscribed 'TLF 1681'. Operated for at least 40 years up to *c.*1830 by the Spark family, it was run from *c.*1840 to the mid-1860s by Edward Emmerson, a lead miner and later agent. Widow Ann Slack, innkeeper up to 1881, was succeeded by blacksmith John Dowson. He remained there until *c.*1900, although the Church Gates may have closed as an inn before then. By 1901, John Lancaster, a corn miller, was living there.

To the left is the three-storey King's Arms Hotel, established in 1687 and bearing a stone plaque reading 'CW JULY 1687'. The King's Arms name became a proud declaration of loyalty after the restoration of the monarchy. It was run by Hedley Beaty (a constable) in the 1830s/40s, then John Nattrass in the 1850s. Around 1860 it was acquired by the long-serving Robert Lee, who developed it into a larger commercial enterprise. He added a coach house, stables and cottages along Thirlwalls Lane to the rear. After his death in 1903, aged 79, it was run for about ten years by son John W., and by 1914 had passed to Nicholas J. Hall.

Grisdale's Lane, a rarely photographed hidden old 'close' or 'backsyde' of Alston – as early records refer to them – is shown on the town plan of 1775. It has, like many others, changed its name several times, but never had a street sign. The area could only be accessed from lower Front Street via three sections of archway beneath buildings, one of which was ancient with mullioned windows. The lane led through two small courtyards and into one larger one, the enclosed area adjoining the vicarage garden wall to the west, and the Maltings and Kates Lane to the south.

In the 1841 census this close is recorded as Edmund's Lane. Prior to 1800 there was an innkeeper called Edmund Bulman in Alston, followed by another, a blacksmith, who died in 1832 aged 66 (his family grave is at Alston). In 1851 it had become Bulman's Lane and was home to 47 residents occupying twelve properties (none were empty). By 1861 it had reverted to Edmund's, increasing to 77 people living in eighteen properties (a further two were empty). This name remained in use until 1891, by which time only 30 residents occupied eleven properties, with seven lying empty.

By 1900 it had become Grisdale's Lane, this name persisting up to the present day, with the occasional use of Vicarage Terrace (pre 1920s) and later Birkett's [bakery site] Lane. In c.1912 there were ten occupied cottages, four warehouses, one stable and a small shop, the latter in the first courtyard, occupied by Michael Brough, butcher. Thirteen of the sixteen properties were owned by William R. Little ('Walton & Little, Wines and Spirits'), who had a shop on the corner of the Front Street entrance. Continued demolition and the post-1950 Church Road developments have since transformed the area.

John Grisdale (born c.1823, Greystoke) rebuilt several of these properties and lived near the Front Street entrance.

He was married to Jane, the daughter of Joseph Edgar, who he initially lodged with. Established as a joiner and builder at Alston in the 1850s/60s (he was under-bidder for the Town Hall contract in 1857), he later moved to Newcastle to expand his business. By 1881 he employed twelve men, dying there in 1884 aged 61.

The 1901 census records 27 residents in the lane, and if this picture was taken around that time it may include the following: Mary Craig (83), Frances Scott (26), Mary Thursby (29), Eleanor Irving (58), Elizabeth Lee (79), Mary Whitfield (77), Sarah Lee (26), Mary A. Whitfield (65), Frances (10), Phyllis (44) and William Green (77). Two lead miners (presumably at work when the photograph was taken) also lived here, which would account for the minerals on the landing and windowsill. Of Alston's two town postmen (there were also three rural ones), John Tatters (43) and John Cousin (26), the latter is probably the one in the picture, while the foreign looking hawker or delivery man, with assorted bottles, remains unidentified.

Second post office site at entrance to Grisdale's Lane. Postmistress Phillis Errington. Advert, *Alston Herald*, May 1874

The Town Hall, seen here in *c*.1886, is an imposing Gothic style building located on a prominent site (donated by Greenwich Hospital) in the old vicarage garden. The building comprised a spacious upper public hall to hold 400, used for a wide range of purposes including meetings, concerts and County Court sessions. Facilities on the ground floor included the Literary & Mechanics' Institute Library, a reading and news room, boardroom (for the Poor Law Guardians), along with registrar's and later District Council offices. The east side annex incorporated the Savings Bank (est. 1825) and a dwelling house.

The architect was A.B. Higham of Wakefield, and in March 1857 four builders tendered for the construction work. Thomas March of Blaydon was successful with an estimate of £1,630, the 'over-bidder' being John Grisdale of Alston, quoting £1,763. Work began on 10 June 1857 and involved 'leading away soil by farmers, 10 to 12 carts employed'. On 15 July the foundation stone (now 'lost'!) was laid by the famous chemist Hugh Lee Pattinson FRS (b.1796, Alston; d.1858, Gateshead), along with a bottle containing artefacts and details of the committee. The opening ceremony took place on 27 December 1858.

The final cost of the main building was about £2,000, raised by public subscription, with an additional *c*.£640 for the Savings Bank paid for out of bank funds. In November 1859 the clock was installed in the tower, but it froze up in December during the first winter storm. The clock was lit by gas which came on at dusk and went off at daybreak.

The Vicarage, seen among the trees to the left, was in very poor condition in the early 1800s. In 1811 the vicar, Revd Benjamin Jackson (who served Alston from 1790 to 1834), agreed to transfer his third of the presentation (patronage) to the Greenwich Hospital (which already held two thirds) in return for a 'comfortable' new building. This was completed in 1812, at a cost of £1,323, and included a cottage, stable and byre.

The 24 foot high monument on the right, made of red (Ross of Mull) and grey (Aberdeen) granite by R. Beall of Newcastle, was inaugurated on 18 November 1864 in 'extremely miserable weather'. It is dedicated to Jacob Walton of Greenends, Nenthead, a well known owner and agent of lead, zinc, copper and coal mines. He died in March 1863, aged 53. The land on which the monument stood, originally leased by the Town Hall trustees in 1875, was purchased for £125 by the County Council in 1939 for road improvements. When these were eventually implemented in 1960, the structure was dismantled and stored, with only the inscribed plaque remaining on site. It was finally reinstated in July 2004.

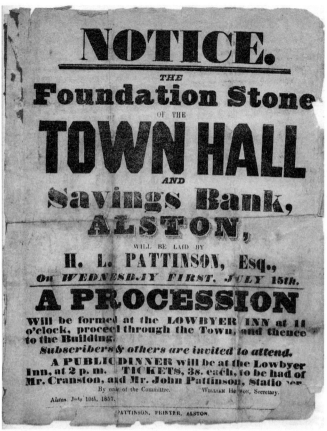

Poster dated 10 July 1857

Advert, *Carlisle Journal*, 1 May 1857

Advert, 1894

Advert, 1882

Advert, 1912

Advert, 1882

Front Street, Alston. SLD.

These buildings facing the Town Hall have changed little since they were photographed *c.*1912. Previously run by Matthew and Elizabeth Graham, the corner grocery and confectionery store, seen below the gable end of the King's Arms Hotel, was taken over by the Hodgson family *c.*1872. Thomas Hodgson was a stone and monumental mason from Ainstable (Cumberland), who later worked on the church tower and spire. He was assisted by son John (b.1861) who had three well-known daughters: Frances (b.1890), who married the Revd N.A. Walton, Vicar of Alston; Gladys (b.1893); and Eva (b.1895), a local teacher. When Thomas died in 1892, aged 56, his wife Frances continued to run the shop, also taking in boarders. She died in 1910, aged 76, after which the premises were acquired by boot and shoemaker Jack (and later Walton) Varty. After the second war it became Bannister's shoe shop.

'White House', adjoining below, was originally the Dun Cow Inn and was managed from the 1820s by Margaret Armstrong, then from the 1850s to the mid-1880s by Greystoke-born joiner William Green (d.1902, aged 78). He was followed by Ann Dowson who remained until the inn's closure in the early 1890s.

The long-serving Dawsons, who were in business from the 1840s, were grocers and game dealers at the third property down. Twice-married Joseph (d.1887, aged 75) was succeeded by his son Johnny who died in 1941, aged 88. The shop was carried on by his daughter 'Winnie' well into the post-war period. She died in 1986, aged 100.

The next building, with flagpole, was originally a double shop and office used by J.&J. Dickinson, solicitors. It also housed the Alston Corps Volunteer club room and drill sergeant's flat (Nicholas Blezard of the Border Regiment

held this post in 1891). The building was subsequently in the hands of the Liberal Club (formed in 1890) as seen here, then became the Comrades Club in the 1920s. It was partly rebuilt *c.*1900, when a single doorway was installed and the upper two storeys reduced to one with the addition of high windows and a dormer. The white passageway provided access to Bank Lane and the Alston Bank (later Freemason's Hall), owned by Joseph Dickinson Sr. from Lovelady Shield and established in 1847. Joseph was one of the last of the private solicitor/bankers when he sold to the Carlisle City & District Bank in 1890. He continued with them as manager until his death in 1895, aged 84. In 1896, the bank became part of the London, City & Midland, moving premises shortly afterwards to the Market Place corner. Jos. Dickinson's clerk, Henry Whitfield, served as manager there from 1896 to 1901. He was succeeded by Watson Sykes (salary £180 pa) until 1911, after which Joseph Spraggon Whitfield (Henry's nephew) took over until 1937. A branch of the Cumberland Union Bank operated briefly (1890–93) from a facing property.

The shop of J. Leake & Son, fruiterer, on the left, had been established by 1910 but was gone by 1920. It was later run as a milliner and fancy draper by Mabel Graham, after which daughter Evelyn took over. In the early 1880s Jacob W. Smith, a draper and grocer from Cowgap Farm, traded from here, retiring in about 1900. He died in 1906, aged 67. From *c.*1903 Joseph Hodgson, butcher and farmer from Bayle Hill, occupied the adjoining basement 'shop' (unseen) next to Spring House.

The lone central figure in the road is James J. Stokes, Greenwich Hospital Receiver and Agent. He lived and worked at the Old Manor House, having arrived in Alston from Kew in 1907, aged 40. He had retired by 1923.

Low Mill was used to grind corn and replaced a ruined water-powered fulling or 'walk' mill, in operation forty to fifty years earlier, where cloth was cleaned before being stretched out to dry on 'tenter' frames. The new corn mill stood on part of the Church Crofts (fields), also known as 'Millers Wifes Brow'. It was built by Thomas Lee and Robert Hodgson after they each acquired half shares of the site in 1761, along with a licence for a road down Tenter Bit field. In 1795 Hodgson acquired the other half share and in 1814, following his death, his executor sold the corn mill and adjoining house to clockmaker Joseph Hall for £740. Following the addition of extra land, property and a garden, the estate was purchased in 1825 by widow Esther Vipond for £1,050. In 1844, after her death, it passed to son Utrick who remained there until c.1863. At the time, in addition to the four-storey mill, there was a house, stables, warehouses and cottages, plus a grocery shop with main road frontage. Tenant Matthew Whitfield purchased the mill complex in 1876 for £1,856, adding an adjacent 'joiner's shop & warehouse plot' in 1888. He died in 1893, aged 63, after which the property passed to his son Samuel. Unmarried and with no children, Samuel died aged 45 in 1903, leaving the mill to his housekeeper Sarah Scaife (52). She immediately sold it to miller William Lee for £1,400.

Hugh Haldon, whose family were originally joiners (later trading as grocers, with a shop and properties nearly opposite), purchased Low Mill in 1912. He was joined by sons William (d.1963, aged 78) and Thomas (d.1974, aged 80) who later ran the grocery store. They operated as millers and corn merchants until the 1950s, after which the main building was demolished c.1964.

FIRST CLASS CORN MILL TO LET.

TO be LET, and may be entered upon immediately, all that excellent WATER CORN MILL, called the LOW MILL, situate at ALSTON, in the County of Cumberland.

The Mill is in excellent order, and capable of grinding sufficient Flour, Meal, &c., for a large district around Alston, in which there is little or no competition. For an enterprising man the present is a most favourable opportunity for establishing a large and remunerative business with a very moderate capital.—For further particulars apply at the office of S. and S. G. SAUL, Solicitors, Carlisle, where tenders may be sent. The highest preferred rent will not necessarily be accepted.

Carlisle, July 8th, 1863.

Advert, *Carlisle Journal*, 24 July 1863

Advert, 1894

Advert, *Carlisle Journal*, 19 March 1858

The Mill Burn did not only provide water to Low Mill. A branch higher up first fed a sawmill run by Thomas Richardson, joiner and millwright. It then ran under Thirlwalls Lane and into the race seen on the lower right of this late 1880s photo by Thomas Bramwell. After feeding a *c.*29 foot overshot waterwheel, which powered the machinery, the tail-race rejoined the main stream at the foot of Burn Bank track. This adjoined the house (hidden by the mill) on Station Road where John and George Tatters began their carriage and livery (later garage) business in the 1880s. The Mill Burn then passed under the road, running through the field opposite, seen in the foreground of the picture on page 70. This later became the site of Alston Moor Auction Mart Ltd. Its establishment in 1918 by auctioneer Adam Elliot (b.1858, brother of Robert, Carlisle & Cumberland Bank manager) and others heralded the demise of the traditional fairs and animal sales held at Fair Hill.

Low Mill ground floor shop, office and loading area with Station Road frontage, c.1964, shortly before demolition

Advert, 1888

ALSTON STATION.

T.W.TATTERS.

This late Victorian photograph shows Alston's compact 'gem of a branch line terminus station', adjacent to the confluence of the Nent and South Tyne Rivers. It was taken by Thos. William Tatters (a stationer and printer whose shop was opposite the church) from his family home adjoining Low Mill. The Newcastle & Carlisle Railway Company branch line from Haltwhistle was authorised by Act of Parliament in 1846 and modified with diversions in 1849. After delays in completing Lambley Viaduct, it opened fully on 17 November 1852, with its associated 'electric telegraph' installed and working by April 1853. The line was taken over by the North Eastern Railway Co. in 1862.

The elegant Jacobean-style buildings, with decorated gables, mullioned windows and tall chimneys, were designed in 1851 by noted Newcastle architect John Green and his son Benjamin. They planned many other fine buildings, including the Theatre Royal in Newcastle. The original 125 foot long arc-roof, which protected the single platform, was supported by the station house and offices to the right and the buttressed wall on the left. When the roof was replaced during improvements in 1872/73, a new mansard style version was installed. This cost £446/13/6d and was bigger than its predecessor, being raised by 16 inches and extended north by 25 feet. The original 12 inch high platform was later raised to 30 inches, requiring steps down into the station rooms.

Having also been enlarged, the adjoining single track, run-through engine shed on the left extended to 85 feet, with a 70 foot inspection pit. Alongside it, with connecting doorways, was the workshop and smithy, as well as stores and a mess room with a 7,000 gallon water tank on the roof. Beyond these, outside, were a water column and wooden coaling platform.

The run-round line to the left, which adjoined the station allotments, linked to the rarely photographed and short-lived shed for snowplough No. 4 (1888). Behind this was the original signal box with timber gable ends. This was replaced in 1905 by a brick hip-roofed version. A 42 foot turntable (out of view below the wall on the extreme right) provided access to the platform, engine shed and run-round lines. Beyond this complex, at the centre of a quite extensive goods yard, was the stone goods shed/warehouse, measuring 70 x 40 feet, seen on the right. This was served by twin sidings (one run-through), with two large arched cart loading bay entrances on the far (east) side.

When the line was merged into the LNER in 1923, the livery of the rolling stock changed from maroon to a sombre brown. The merger also heralded a slow decline in branch traffic, with goods services withdrawn in September 1965. By this time the canopy, engine shed and other buildings had been demolished. After several reprieves, the line closed completely on Saturday 1 May 1976 after 124 years of operation. Two days later, on 3 May, Viscount Ridley formally opened the new so-called 'all weather' road.

The last scheduled steam-hauled passenger train to Alston ran on 27 September 1959, but steam still continued to work goods after that date.

The following diary entry includes brief additions from an accompanying letter, which also makes reference to barrels of free 'barley bree' given to the railway navvies, resulting in many 'friendly pugilistic encounters'!

5 January 1852

The long expected day for opening the Alston Branch of Railway arrived, the New Band left Alston at 7 o'clock for the terminus where a truck was prepared. It was drawn by a horse [1½ miles] to Gilderdale where the Alston Engine were waiting their arrival, then they proceeded to Lambley [8½ miles from Alston] where a party of the Railway Co. gentlemen & others met them, the Band played at intervals all the way back to Alston where many people with flags, deafening cheers of the crowd, tolling of bells and roars of cannon met the arrival of the first Locomotive Engine that ever came to Alston. Many had never heard the shrill screech of the whistle nor the snort or puff of the engine. The Train consisted of the Engine and tender, two passenger Carriages, a low truck with the Band, and last 10 waggons of coals. The coals were given to the poor carried by 10 horses and Carts, the horses had rosettes at each ear with ribands. (the first fruits of a Railway, Charity Coals for the poor). The ten Carts of Coals were preceded by the Band to the Lock up, [Police Station at Townhead] where the band stood in front till the Coals were tip't or emptied, then the carts returned for more.

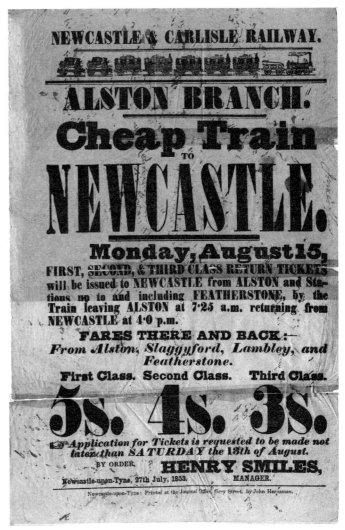

Poster, 27 July 1853

Auctioneer Adam Elliot (photo Dix & Smedley c.1878)

Alston Moor Auction Mart share certificate, 1918

There were few accidents on the heavily engineered 13-mile Alston line which incorporated sixty numbered viaducts, bridges and culverts. The service, which usually terminated at Haltwhistle for connections to Newcastle and Carlisle ('through running' only occurred occasionally) kept excellent time, with many locals setting their clocks or watches by passing trains. There were initially two trains daily in each direction, but the number had increased to three by the 1870s and four by 1900. In the years before the Second World War there were up to six (excluding Sundays, goods traffic and workmen's/miners' specials). By the 1880s the original 40 minute journey had been reduced to about 35 minutes.

In the later nineteenth century, working by former main line engines gave way to branch line classes, and by 1900 Bogie Tank Passenger (BTP) 0-4-4T engines were in regular use. Introduced in 1874 and designed by E. Fletcher for local passenger work, some 124 of these were built. They included No. 69, seen here in 1920 being retrieved from the River South Tyne at Alston by a steam crane. Whilst secondary sources suggest the locomotive was unattended at the time of the early morning incident, a first-hand account tells a different story. It claims that a careless cleaner, whose duties also included coaling and watering the engines, had accidentally over-filled the boiler, and on moving from the shed it 'caught the water'. He was unable to close the regulator and the locomotive ran away. Having been diverted by trap points near the signal box (designed to protect the running lines), BTP 69 careered off the rails into Station Pool, landing on its bunker. The badly damaged engine was taken to Gateshead Yards where it was noted awaiting repair in June 1920.

As Lambley Viaduct was unfinished, the Alston Branch line could only carry goods traffic via the Brampton Railway when it officially opened on 5 January 1852. The euphoric events of the day were marred by human tragedy. Three Slaggyford boys, riding on the coal and slate wagons of the second train up, were thrown off when it 'jerked' on entering the station. One badly injured his arm, while another, Joseph Teasdale, required the amputation of both his crushed feet and died the next morning. The same day, the passenger stagecoach connecting with trains at Lambley overturned at Thornhope Bridge (where a railway navvy had died a year earlier). Driver Thos. Kirkley was 'much hurt'. Later fatalities included Joseph Vevers, who fell on wagon couplings in August 1852; Arthur Seely (painter), who fell from the station roof in 1879; and John Teasdale who died loading timber in 1898.

The other accident of note on the Alston line involved the derailment of the 2 p.m. train to Haltwhistle on Saturday 22 March 1947. It took place near Gilderdale, and this photograph by keen Alston photographer 'Ernie' Barber appeared in the *Cumberland & Westmorland Herald*. The derailment tore up a long length of track, but there were no serious injuries to the estimated two dozen passengers on board. However, newlyweds David Edgar (later of The Dyke, Kirkhaugh) and his bride Vera (née Macmillan), were particularly disappointed, as they had been on their way to Blackpool for their honeymoon.

The accident was caused by the combined failure of 'life expired' sleepers and frost damaged track after the long harsh winter. The 0-6-0 'J39' class engine had been running tender first, as the Alston turntable was damaged and out of use. Despite having left the rails it remained upright, as did the second and third carriages. The first tipped on its side and its occupants were rescued by loco fireman Bert Harrison of Alston. Minor injuries were treated by Dr Hassan, who arrived on the footplate of the 'spare' Alston engine, sent by stationmaster Bill Ruddick. The accident scene is recalled by (then) youngsters Jack Douglas, who was travelling to Miss Snowballs (Haltwhistle) for piano lessons and Audrey Fawcett (later Davison) going shopping with her father. Here passenger Bob Sproat (a railway linesman) is seen walking away from colleagues 'Willie' Hudspith (left), a guard and landlord of the George & Dragon in Garrigill, Ned Dickinson (linesman, Alston), and right, Tom Morton (linesman, Slaggyford). The driver, unseen and unhurt, was Tommy Stannard of Alston.

A surprisingly cheerful group of 'rescued' passengers who obviously don't need trauma counselling!

RAILWAY STATION, ALSTON

This panoramic view across the River Nent was taken in the mid-1890s and shows the gasworks and Hexham road, with the 1851 station building beyond. The latter was extended between 1904 and 1908 with the addition of a scullery and store to the left gable, plus booking office, porters' room and gents to far north end. To the right (east) and further north, were extensive goods traffic facilities, with special provision for loading limestone (c.25,000 tons in 1923) and ore. Following the decline in lead mining after 1870, zinc became the principal ore traffic with, for example, about 9,000 tons being despatched c.1910. The wide platform area (seen at centre) was raised up 4½ feet to enable direct cart loading and was also fitted with a four ton crane. Lengthy sidings at the station, which included livestock facilities, held up to 150 wagons. A similar number could also be accommodated at four sidings to the north where the Alston Lime Co., Alston & Nent Force Quarry Co. and Vieille Montagne Zinc Co. had private loading facilities. A further extension, added in 1908, ran between the goods shed and the double-track coal depot, seen on the right. This passed under the A686 road through tunnel No. 61 into the Nent Force limestone quarry, where there was a loading bay for stone. About 30 staff, including loco and track maintenance workers, were based at Alston station.

When the first stationmaster William Little retired c.1878 after nearly 27 years, residents presented him with 'several valuable articles worth £35'. He was succeeded by Joseph Walton (ex head clerk) until c.1900, followed by John Railton

to c.?1920, then Joseph Little. Mr Ruddick and Mr Crags held the post after the Second World War, with William Wood taking over from c.1955. He was replaced by Mr Summers in the early 1960s.

Although mains electricity was not available until 1934, the Alston Gas Light & Coke Co. (formed in 1842) first lit the town with gas from the works in the foreground in May 1843. Here, coal was burned in retorts to produce 'town gas', coke and tar. With no direct rail link, incoming coal supplies crossed the road by horse and cart, with even the later 1908 quarry siding only loading outgoing 40 gallon tar barrels. In 1911, when the business became a limited company, the works had two gasometers with capacities of 9,500 and 1,800 cubic feet. Equipment included a six-unit retort plant, two purifiers, six double condensers, a tar tank and a meter house, along with the office and manager's house. It was later taken over by Hexham Gas Co., which was nationalised in 1948, becoming part of the Northern Gas Board. Production at Alston ceased in 1960, and the gasworks was replaced by a butane plant. This was supplied by road deliveries until Alston was connected to North Sea Gas in 1987, after which the works were dismantled. Managers included: first Ralph Smith, serving into the 1860s; William Walton c.1870–90 (the brother of photographer Hugh, he emigrated to Australia and died in 1895, aged 53); Joseph H. Pickering up to about the First World War; then Fred Nicholson, who remained in post until c.1939.

Scant records and frequent changes in proprietors and tenants make piecing together the history of the woollen mill difficult. Although a major employer in the town, the mill had a chequered career and 'proved an unfortunate speculation to most of the owners'. It was built as a flax and cotton (not woollen!) spinning mill in 1799 by William

---

ALSTON MILL, CUMBERLAND.

TO be LET, and entered upon immediately, the Premises known as the ALSTON WOOLLEN or WORSTED MILL, situate at ALSTON, in the County of Cumberland, with the recently built DWELL-ING HOUSE, and about 4A. 3R. 10P. of LAND adjoining thereto, and occupied therewith.

The Mill is four storeys high, and measures 108 feet in length by 30ft. 6in. in breadth, and the Machinery is driven by an abundant supply of water power.   It is replete with Machinery for preparing, Combing, and Spinning Worsted Yarns, and Weaving the same. There are Stove, Skin, and Boiler Houses, Dye House, Sulphur House, Warehouse, and Counting House adjoining, and all conveniently situated.   The Mill is in a district offering advantages for securing clips of wool of the finest description, and is in close proximity to the Alston Station of the Newcastle and Carlisle section of the North Eastern Railway.   It would make an excellent Corn or Paper Mill.

The Dwelling House is within 200 yards of the Mill, and is suitable for the residence of an owner or manager.

Proposals to be forwarded to Messrs. BAINBRIDGE and MILLICAN, Solicitors, Alston, Cumberland, who will send a person to show the premises, and give all further information.

Todd, who also leased the High Mill (corn). He allowed the Congregationalists and their Sunday School to use a large room for meetings until a new chapel was built in 1804 on nearby land gifted by him.

Todd continued to operate the mill himself after attempting to secure tenants in 1802. He sold it to John Lowry of Carlisle in 1812, who leased it out the following year. The four-storey stone building measured 81 x 37 feet and housed the latest flax (linen) spinning machinery. It was powered by a large water wheel fed from an underground culvert, which was 'never known to freeze'. The building was fireproofed, with features including cast-iron columns and a large top floor river-fed reservoir for 'instant inundation'. It was heated throughout by steam pipes. In 1822 it was occupied by 'John Atkins & others' and offered for sale as a 'Flax Manufactory with dwellinghouse and 4 acres of Land'. By 1825 the range of activities carried out there included 'carding, spinning, dying wool and weaving coarse woollen cloths and flannels'. William Atkin was the occupant in 1828, while in the 1830s Thomas Bentley (flax spinners and linen manufacturers) added shoe and sewing thread to the list of products. Thomas died in 1838, aged 35, and during the 1840s his relatives, Smith, Stobart & Co., employed around 80 people at the 'extensive worsted mill', by now five storeys high.

Next to run the mill were the Nenthead based family of Robert Walton & Co. Robert died in 1849, aged 35, and in 1851 63 employees were working at the mill. In 1860 it was

continued overleaf

Advert, *Carlisle Journal*, 19 June 1868

leased to Whitewall, Busher & Co. of Kendal, who employed 26 people in 1861. Failed attempts to let the mill in 1868 led to the formation of Alston Carpet & Woollen Co. Ltd. in 1870 (share capital £8,000). By then the main building had been extended to 108 feet, with a new 'Factory House' (later renamed Nentholme) added nearby. The owner of the mill, J.P. Walton of Greenends, was one of the new company's six directors. Its prospectus described advantages including good wool and water supplies, cheap labour and close railway links. Of the 55 employed in 1871, 50 per cent were from outside Alston. They included fourteen carpet weavers, among whom were five Scots, four from Kendal and three from Yorkshire.

In the mid-1870s the mill was bought by Akerigg Bros. of Kendal, three of whom lived locally. A fire in May 1877 caused £500 of damage, followed by another 'very destructive' blaze in July 1878, after which about £13,000 was spent rebuilding the mill, but at a reduced height. In the early 1880s 40–50 people were employed there, although the company later went into liquidation. The machinery was auctioned off in May 1889, after which the factory lay unoccupied.

Although purchased by the quarry company in 1908 for the installation of a crushing plant, the main buildings, seen here looking south-east c.1920s, remained empty. They were finally acquired in the 1930s by builder brothers Tom and Fred Kearton. Through links with their third brother Hugh, a director of Sunderland crane makers Steel Co. Ltd. (later Coles Cranes), the Alston Foundry Co. Ltd. was formed as a subsidiary at the outbreak of the Second World War. The old mill, described as 'isolated from aerial bombardment', was converted into a munitions works producing 3 inch mortar bomb casings, which were then sent to Oldham for filling

with explosives. Known as the 'Bottom Factory' it operated two iron furnaces, two Bessemer steel converters and six casting tables. It was managed by Sheffield metallurgist Tom Hunter, assisted by Jim Murphy under chairman Eric Steel. The workforce of farmers and women produced about 6,000 shells per week, managing 20,000 during their 'Jackpot Week'. In total around a million bomb cases were made. The factory went on to produce 20-link, 60 foot long 'boom defence mooring chains' which protected against submarines and were designed for the D-Day landings etc. Having survived the war and employing up to 200 people, the specialist casting foundry finally closed in 1980. Managing director Frank Allinson reopened the factory on a much scaled down basis as Falmech, but it closed again in 1989.

There are only two known photographs (both taken *c.*1900) of the original entrance to the Nent Force Level, which was later obliterated by limestone quarrying. This famous eighteenth century engineering feat is shrouded in mystery and myth. Described as a 'Stupendous Work', it was probably the largest and most expensive lead mining project in the North Pennines. Completion of the initial tunnel (approximately five miles in length) took 63 years and cost more than £80,000. It was engineered by the two Greenwich Hospital Estates Receivers (managing agents), John Smeaton (of Eddystone Lighthouse fame) and Nicholas Walton (born *c.*1732, Alston), who was local chief agent from 1758 until his death in 1810.

The purpose of the venture was to discover new mineral veins up the Nent Valley and drain the ground above. Work commenced in June 1776 near the Nent Force waterfall, below Alston. It was begun as a 'horse' level, measuring 3½ feet wide by 7 feet high, a then recent innovation with horses hauling small carriages on rails. At the suggestion of John Gilbert, the Duke of Bridgewater's visiting agent, the size of the level was increased in June 1777 to 8 feet square. This allowed the formation of an underground canal that could carry *c.*12 ton capacity boats. It was twenty-nine years later, in 1805, when the first section (measuring 2.2 miles and costing £26,000) was finally flooded to a depth of four feet. When it was tried out with boats, however, the method proved uneconomical. Having extended the canal section to 3.43 miles, and with only one workable vein discovered, the boat level was terminated at Nentsberry Shaft (360 feet deep) in 1824.

The drive continued up valley 150 feet nearer the surface as a horse level. Many obstacles were overcome, including hard rock and excessive water (which meant that explosives had to be encased in tin canisters), only to discover that the major Nenthead veins were barren in depth. As a result the main drive ended in 1839, with a connection made to Brewery Shaft (328 feet deep), the last of nine air/access shafts along its length, in 1842. A large stone plaque, erected at the entrance and removed when quarrying began, is now in the Town Hall foyer. The term 'folly' is often used to describe this bold but fruitless venture, which continues to drain the Nent Valley mine complex. It has spawned numerous nostalgic tales of exciting Victorian boat trips by both locals and visitors alike, although this vision wasn't shared by writer J.W. Allan in 1878. He described the monotony of his weird, unearthly, depressing boat journey ('candles stuck all round the sides'), which was only relieved by the sounds of a concertina playing, the piteous howling of a bulldog, and pistol shots. He later emerged chilled, wet and cramped from the 'unhealthy drain'!

The Alston Moor estates were controlled from two important Greenwich Hospital buildings a short distance up the Hexham road. Lowbyer 'New' Manor House, on the east (right) side, was rebuilt and enlarged in 1778 as the (Golden) Anchor Inn. Described as 'a capital mansion', it provided superior accommodation and business facilities for mine owners and agents. By 1890 it was the home of J.R. Walton, civil/mining engineer and JP. Close by on the other side of the road was the ancient 'Old' Manor House. This was originally used by the Earl of Derwentwater's stewards, and Manorial Courts were held there until 1925. After 1735 it became the Greenwich Hospital Moormaster and bailiff's official residence and office, closing c.1946.

Loaning Foot House, seen here in 1890, stands opposite the Old Manor House at the junction with North (originally Lowbyer) Loaning, facing on to Thirlwall's Field. This was previously the home of Greenwich Hospital mine agent Adam Walton, who retired in 1887. When the photograph was taken it was leased to William Hall Jr. (b.1850, brother of Harrison Hall, saddler), who like his father was a long-serving coal agent (Evanwood and Coanwood collieries etc.). He had a depot at the station and was also a cattle dealer and carter. His wife Jane (b.1849) seen in the gateway, let 'apartments' (rooms) which were frequented by visiting cyclists. Several other early photos of cyclists are posed here. In about 1900 the Halls moved back up to Townhead (Cross Fell View, Chapel Terrace). Mary Nicholson then moved into Loaning Foot House, offering 'furnished apartments'.

Alston was a popular destination for cycle touring clubs, and of the five cyclists seen above two are locals (in dark jackets), while the other three are visitors. All are wearing plus fours, caps and lapel badges, and are seen meeting friends. The group are, from the left: Doig on a cross-frame safety bicycle; Appleby on a diamond-frame safety model;

and Thomas William Tatters (22) of Townfoot, Alston, a draper's assistant and later printer and stationer with a shop opposite the church (d.1938, aged 71). Next along is Thomas Lattimer (24) a grocer and draper of Nenthead; then Thomas Hornsby (26) farmer of High Lovelady Shield on a penny farthing (correct name 'ordinary'); followed by Mrs Jane Hall (41); and Tom Bell (24), a machinist in Elswick, Newcastle, from an Alston family, on a cross-frame safety. Behind him and slightly obscured is Joseph Graham (35) blacksmith of Nenthead; then A. Scott, possibly from the farming family of Blagill, Alston; and C. Lamb on the rarer facile bicycle (a variation of an 'ordinary', available from c.1888). All the models are 'fixed-wheel', with solid rubber tyres which were bought in coils and cut to length. The bicycles have touring bags attached and 'spoon' brakes, while four include lamps and 'free-wheeling' front fork foot rests.

This Edwardian photograph shows Newshieldbank Toll House, situated north of the town on the present A686 road. It features a viewing window in its south gable. By the mid-eighteenth century a crude and irregular road ran from Penrith to Hexham through Alston, the eastern portion of which was turnpiked in 1778. Together with the Alston branch of the Lobley Hill Turnpike, this was the only other improved route in existence until the 1820s. Facing the Randleholme junction (left), Newshieldbank was probably built in 1824. The original 1778 toll bar had been at Lowbyer Old Manor House where it controlled both the main and North Loaning roads.

In 1822 the Greenwich Hospital directors requested a report (published in 1823) from Secretary E.H. Locker on the 'State and Condition of the Roads and Mines' on their extensive northern estates. Mr Locker commissioned the famous John Loudon MacAdam, who surveyed the main routes within a 36 mile radius of Alston. He found them to be in 'a deplorable state', badly aligned and poorly constructed. This was particularly problematic because, as he noted 'the articles produced in the country … are of a heavy description, viz: Lead & Lead Ore [14,000 tons] Coal, Lime, Timber, Stone … making an aggregate carried of 20,000 tons per ann.'. He recommended that the existing Alston to Hexham turnpike be linked to five other branch routes, a plan that would involve 126 miles of new and improved roads being made at a cost of £26,000.

Formed by an 1824 Act of Parliament, the large Alston Turnpike Trust incorporated the roads of the two existing trusts in the area. It was supported by generous subscriptions from Greenwich Hospital (£5,000), the London Lead Co. (£5,000), Hudgill Burn Co. (£3,000) and other mine owners. Much of the work had been completed by 1830, and the first post coach, 'The Balloon', commenced service between Hexham, Alston and Penrith on 29 September 1828. Like many other turnpike trusts, Alston's was in debt for most of its existence, but survived until it was disbanded in 1875, when the 'main' roads came under county control. The turnpike trustees sold the trust's properties at Mark Close, Langley (Allendale), Newshieldbank and Loaning Head to Greenwich Hospital for £165 in March 1876.

Five other toll houses existed in the Alston area, one of which remains on the Blagill road at the head of nearby North Loaning. It was built in 1824 and is of a similar design to Langley Castle and Langwathby tolls. At the time the road ran in front of the surviving property, not behind it as it does now. Toll houses at Hartside Gate (Penrith road), Skelgill (Weardale road), Mark Close (Brampton road) and West Nattrass (Teesdale road), have long since been demolished.

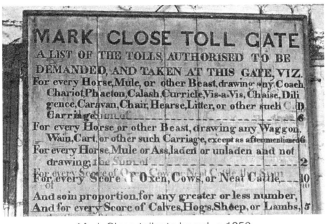

Mark Close tollgate board, c.1850

Holmes' Foot and St. Patrick's Well, Alston

This outcrop of Scar Limestone at Cats-Scar was reached from the Hexham road by a pleasant walk of two-thirds of a mile, along the east bank of the South Tyne. On leaving the road opposite Loaning Foot House at Waif Garth Field, the route crossed the foot of Coatlith Limeworks railway incline, then passed Holms nurseries and Turnwheel Bridge, before reaching this picturesque place. Victorian ladies, like the one seen here *c.*1900, could 'while the restful hours away' and drink spring water from the chained iron cup at 'St' Patrick's Well. This facility was named after its provider, Irishman Patrick Gilmore, a popular local character but no saint!

The burgeoning nineteenth century interest in natural history included the collecting of mineral specimens by wealthy individuals, institutions and museums. Many of these highly prized specimens were sourced from North Pennine lead mines. Long-established Alston mineral dealers included the Cowper family, who were also grocers, jewellers and 'lapidaries'. John Sr. was previously a Garrigill miner 'with little ambition to advance beyond his class'. However, encouraged by his wife Sarah (d.1859, aged *c.*79), 'a woman superior to her position', he went on to run shops at Alston and Keswick. Also involved were sons Emerson (d.1863, aged 56) a grocer, 'mineralogist and lead ore agent', and enterprising John Jr. (d.1875, aged 64) who partnered Jacob Walton in many mining ventures (lead, coal and iron). From the 1820s William Burrow operated as a mineral dealer until his death in 1877, aged 88. The business in the Butts was then continued by his assistant (from *c.*1870) John Jones, who last appears as a 'mineralogist' aged 65, in the 1891 census.

The most notable local dealer was resourceful Patrick Gilmore (born *c.*1834). He was a shepherd's son from Ballygar (Galway, Ireland) who arrived at Alston in 1857 with his first wife Jane (d.1866, aged 28) and son Peter (b.1856, Carlisle). The family lived in the upper Butts where Patrick operated as a ragman, hawker and mineral dealer. Assisted by Peter (who later 'took to the drink') and second wife Elizabeth (born *c.*1843, Carlisle; married 1866), he developed an extensive trade in mineral specimens, selling to collectors, wholesale dealers and institutions. The British Museum was amongst his many influential customers and he also sold to Europe and the USA. Notable American collector, lawyer Charles H. Pennypacker, who visited in 1889, spent three days examining the Gilmores' stock. Later, describing banker and fellow mineralogist William Jefferis's trip to Alston, he wrote, 'The set out of specimens in that old warehouse was so intoxicating that fifty English sovereigns disappeared in short order. Such temptations could not be resisted'. Patrick's second wife Elizabeth died in 1886, aged 43 and he never remarried. He is described in his will of September 1891 (in which he left £654) as a 'marine store dealer' (scrap and second-hand goods). Patrick acquired many properties in the Butts, including a shop, warehouse, two houses and nine cottages. His son Peter died on 19 September 1892, aged 36, and Patrick, then also the proprietor of the Greyhound Inn, collapsed and died at his funeral aged 58. His estate, including Gilmore House, where he lived, was auctioned in July 1893, raising £605. The house, which included a study and office fitted out with specimen cabinets, fetched £125. Peter's widow, also called Elizabeth (b.1860, Alston), described as a 'shopkeeper', continued to sell minerals until her marriage to carter John Milburn in 1898. The family lived at Back o' the Burn.

Patrick was probably related to Patrick Sarsfield Gilmore (b.1829, Ballygar, emigrated US 1849, lived in Boston, d.1892), and possibly even visited him. He was an illustrious band leader (described as 'Father of the American Band'), concert organiser and successful composer who wrote the Civil War song *When Johnny Comes Marching Home*.

Advert 1882

Patrick Gilmore, *c*.1874

Patricks Well Alston

property, situated in the Butts, belonging to the late Patrick Gilmore. The property was offered at the Greyhound Inn. Messrs Joel and Parsons, Newcastle, acted for the vendors. Lot 1: Fully-licensed leasehold inn, known as the Greyhound, was sold to Mr T. Snowdon for £145. Lot 2: Dwelling house, formerly occupied by the late Patrick Gilmore, £125, Mr T. Place. Lot 3: Four cottages, yard, stone-built warehouse, wood shed, £112 10s, Mr Place. Lot 4: Three cottages, £61, Mr R. Martindale. Lot 5: Byre, barn, and yard, £47 10s, Mr T. Spark. Lot 6: House and shop and two cottages, £85, Mr W. Laws. Lot 7: Close of garden ground, £29, Mr T. Spark. *1893 July*

Report on auction of late Patrick Gilmore's property in the Butts, including Gilmore House and the Greyhound Inn. 'July 1893', source unknown.

Spring water piped into well rock basin, with iron drinking cup on chain, *c*.1905

Looking south in 1905 across the ever dangerous Townfoot junction towards the Golden Lion Hotel. In 1939, part of the old vicarage garden, originally leased from Greenwich Hospital in 1875 by the Town Hall trustees, was purchased by the council for road widening. The area included the Walton Memorial, tennis court and seating. The corner just seen on the left, removed in 1960, housed the Low Well (trough and tap), a post box and an old milestone. The roadworks that had prompted the purchase in 1939 were delayed by the Second World War.

The building on the right with the double outside stairs was Alston's first Wesleyan Methodist Chapel. This was built in 1760, but superseded by a larger building at Back o' the Burn in 1797. The original chapel was then sold to Mr Bustin for £55 and converted into a house and shop for his son-in-law, clockmaker Joseph Hall. Since at least the 1830s, the white property adjoining to the left had included a grocery and confectionery shop. Widow Hannah Bell ran this from the 1850s until her death in 1895 (aged 70), after which her only son Hugh took over until c.1905 (he was also Alston's assistant overseer and registrar). Confectioners Thomas and then Elizabeth Stephenson followed, while in the 1920s Tom and Ethel Fawcett, who added a small tea-room, were the proprietors. By 1934 their successor was the well known Dorothy Fortune from Sunderland, who had previously run a guest house at Kirkhaugh (Temple House). She traded as 'Tweenwhiles' (refreshments), later rebranding as 'Nana Fortune's Toffee Shop' which continued to trade into the early 1970s, albeit with 'irregular' opening hours. The next building to the left was originally the home of land surveyor Joseph Dickinson (d.1853) and his notable daughter Ruth Lancaster (later Ruth Lancaster James). For roughly thirty years until his death in 1911, Henry Whitfield also lived here. Born at Lambley in 1830, he was a long serving cashier

and clerk with J.&J. Dickinson, solicitors and bankers, going on to become manager of the Midland Bank (from where he retired in 1901). After the First World War the premises were used by dentist John Storey as his surgery. He succeeded his father, Thomas James Storey, who practised at nearby Temple Croft. Postman John Tatters lived in the adjoining property (with the bay window), while the Gills occupied the detached house (Dale View) beyond. In the late 1920s this became a private hotel and tea rooms, and much later 'The Cumberland'.

The crowd seen here in June 1905 had gathered for the annual long distance walking race. To their disappointment, only four competitors (in white at the centre) took part. J. Armstrong, who began 'staggering' on a hill seven miles away, went on to win 'on receiving some refreshments and getting well rubbed down', with J. Fawcett taking second place.

'Nana' Fortune in her sweet shop, 1971

This extremely rare photograph shows a group of Alston Mountain Rifle Volunteers assembled at Tyne Willows. It was taken *c.*1885, probably by Thomas Bramwell. The commanding officer was Captain Joseph Dickinson Jr., seen at centre, who had been CO since 1871. He was supported by lieutenants T.W. Dickinson (later honorary major) and W.A. Akerigg, with sergeants J. Pattinson, H.L. Dickinson, W. Hymers, I. Walton and J. Akerigg. The drill instructor was Chelsea Pensioner, Sgt. Henry Reed. Although only fifteen 'rank and file' are shown here, in 1894 they numbered 78. Most of this group are in full dress uniform, the men wearing scarlet tunics with white piped edges, collars and cuffs, along with dark blue trousers. The new style home service pattern spiked helmets were probably dark green. The two lieutenants (foreground left and right) are dressed in patrol jackets with forage caps. The men are armed with single shot breech loading Martini-Henry rifles.

A 'National Volunteer Force' providing defensive support to the regular army, was established in 1859/60. It was made up of unpaid part-time soldiers, with volunteer companies set up on a county basis. The Alston Rifle Volunteers were the sixth of eleven volunteer rifle units raised in Cumberland, with their group HQ first at Carlisle and after 1865 at Keswick. Other units included Penrith Inglewood Forest, Keswick Skiddaw Grey and Brampton Belted Will Rifles. Most of the money for uniforms and equipment was raised by local subscription at events such as dances and bazaars (one in September 1862 raised £264).

The 6th Corps (Alston) Rifle Volunteers (the 'Alston Mountain Rifles' or sometimes 'Alston Mountaineers') first mustered in public on Friday 1 June 1860. They wore light grey uniforms of cloth made from black and white natural sheep's wool. After carrying out drill exercises, the corps marched to the Town Hall to be enrolled, accompanied by the Garrigill Band. Later on they dined at the Golden Lion Inn. The first officers were Captain Commandant Thomas Wilson of Shotley Hall, Lieutenant Joseph Dickinson Sr. and Ensign John Friend. Four sergeants and four corporals were elected, along with Dr Stewart Carson as honorary surgeon and Revd W.N. Snowe (Vicar of Alston) as chaplain. George Law was the 'trumpeter' (bugler). The Dickinson family, solicitors, were long-term supporters, providing premises for the Volunteer room and sergeant's flat. Members of the family also served from 1860–1901, with Joseph Sr. and Joseph Jr. both commanding officers and captains, and Thomas W. a major in later years.

In 1880 the 6th Corps (Alston) became 'I Company' when the various Cumberland units were consolidated into the 1st Cumberland Rifle Volunteers. Later they were incorporated into a volunteer battalion of the Border Regiment, a regular army unit based at Carlisle. The Volunteers formed into the Territorial Force in 1908, which became the Territorial Army in 1921.

Alston Mountaineer Rifles 6th Corps buckle badge

Views of the Golden Lion, located on the west side of Townfoot, are scarce, while those of the Blue Bell and Hillcrest (Alston House) Hotels opposite are common. Seen here c.1910, the Golden Lion's name is heraldically linked to the Percys, Dukes of Northumberland. The inn is noted on maps of 1773/75, when it was owned by William Walton. By 1790 it was described as a 'principal inn' fronting the 'King's High Street'. In 1806 it was purchased by John Little for £315, and when sold to Messrs Wilson, Lee, Crawhall and Nevin in 1836 it comprised three storeys with thirteen rooms, plus two cottages, stabling for twelve horses and extensive cellars. Later, three fields below, originally used as kitchen garden and orchards, were added to the property. Subsequently these became one pasture of 3.3 acres known as 'Lion Bottom', which together with the adjoining Tyne Willows fields were used for Alston show and various sporting events. The property passed via Frederica Milne in 1888 to Mrs M.A. Little, wife of W.R. Little, wine and spirit merchant in 1890. It was leased to Arthur Mann in 1923 and extensively refurbished with a 'dining room for 60 persons'. Having been sold to the McMath family in 1927 (also owners

of the Hillcrest), both properties were conveyed to Lion Hotels Ltd. in 1946, then purchased by Hammond Breweries in 1950. Landlords included William and Margaret Dodd (1820s–50s), Thomas Bushby (1850s–70s), William Hymer (1870s–80s), Stobbs, Harper, Walmsley, Hunter (1880s–1904), Michael Laidlaw, seen in the photograph (1905–c.1912) and John Denwood up to 1923. Following the hotel's demolition c.1959, Hammond's sold the bottom field to Alston Rural District Council for use as a recreation and sports area.

Alston House, situated opposite, is a large multi-phase development which has been home to several prominent landowners. Noted in manorial records in 1690 as being owned by Thos. Lee, by 1773 it was held by Daniel Coats. In 1798 it was bequeathed by Thos. Hall to his granddaughter Elizabeth who married John Leathart. It passed to Robert Hodgson and then in 1823 to Jacob Wilson (d.1858), who largely rebuilt it. In 1867 Jacob's son Thomas (of Bywell) sold it to his nephew, Thos. Wilson Crawhall, for £750. He died in 1892 and his daughter-in-law disposed of it in 1900 to Newcastle ironfounder John Tweddle JP for £600. Tweddle purchased the adjacent Vicarage Field and added a 'spacious bowling green' with its own club, also converting the main building into a guest house for thirty people. Renamed the 'Hillcrest', it went bankrupt in 1910. Richard Welford of Newcastle (possibly a relative), managing director of the Tyne Steam Shipping Co., a notable historian and author, bought the equity for £1,700. Used as a dwelling (partly by himself, the remainder leased to Mrs Reid), he later offered it for sale. After Richard's death in 1919 it was purchased by A.&E. Tench (carriers & carters of Blaydon). They reopened it to guests and in 1923 sold it to the McMaths, noted above.

GOLDEN LION HOTEL, ALSTON.

First-class Family and Commercial. Superior Accommodation, with Moderate Charges. **Private Entrance.** Three Minutes from Station.

WINES, SPIRITS, BEER, &c., OF THE BEST QUALITY.

Posting in all its branches.

JAMES HARPER, Proprietor.

GOLDEN LION

FAMILY & COMMERCIAL HOTEL

.. ¡ALSTON.¡ ..

Three Minutes' Walk from Railway Station.

Every Accommodation for Tourists and Commercial Men.

COMMERCIAL, SITTING AND BED ROOMS

TERMS MODERATE.

Post Horses, Good Stabling, Lock-up Coach Houses, Pleasant Grounds, Lawn Tennis, Fishing &c., &c.

ELLEN WALMSLEY,

PROPRIETRESS.

Advert, 1894

PARTICULARS OF
"HILLCREST," ALSTON, CUMBERLAND.

Suitable for Hydo, Convalescent Home, or Private Residence.

FOR SALE.

STONE BUILT HOUSE.

Entrance Hall, with capacious Porch.
Dining, Drawing and Living Rooms.
Two Kitchens, with ample cooking appliances.
Cloak Room, with Lavatory.
Fourteen Bedrooms and two Attics.
Two Baths, and four W.C.'s
Three Cellars, Scullery, etc.
Billiard Room for full table.
Gas and hot and cold water throughout. Water free—no water rate.
Complete modern drainage.
Large Bowling Green and a Croquet Lawn.
Large walled-in Garden, well planted with fruit trees, etc.

STANDS IN TWO ACRES OF GROUND, ALL FREEHOLD.   FACING MAIN ROAD TO PENRITH

PRICE £1,600, or near offer.

Apply to Owner, R. WELFORD,
Gosforth,
Newcastle-upon-Tyne.

Hillcrest sale particulars, c.WWI

ALSTON ATHLETIC GAMES.

THE Committee of the ALSTON ATHLETIC SOCIETY have great pleasure in announcing that the ANNUAL GAMES will be held in a field near the RAILWAY STATION, *on Whit Monday, 25th May,* 1874.

£15 !
Will be Given in Prizes.

PROGRAMME—Commencing at half-past Twelve o'Clock.

WRESTLING, £5 5s. for 11 Stone Men. Entrance, One Shilling Each.

HANDICAP FOOT RACE, 120 Yards, £5 5s. Entrance, One Shilling Each. To commence at a quarter-past One o'clock precisely.

All entries Post, except the 120 yards Handicap, for which entries must be sent to the Treasurer not later than Monday, the 18th May.

Prizes will also be given for a variety of other games.

Band of the 6th Cumberland Rifle Volunteers on the Ground.

Tea and Refreshments provided by Mr William Hymers, Golden Lion Inn, in the New Marquee.

Mr HUGH PATTINSON, Treasurer.
Mr. W. LITTLE, } Hon.
Mr. W. R. LITTLE, } Secretaries.

Advert, *Alston Herald*, 23 May 1874

BLUE BELL HOTEL. Fully licensed. Family and Commercial. Listed R.A.C. Garage. Motors for Hire. Petrols and Oils.— N. J. Hall, Proprietor.

THE GOLDEN LION HOTEL. Entirely re-furnished and re-decorated throughout. Café and Restaurant. Dining Room to seat 60 persons; separate tables. Private Dining Rooms to seat 10 and 6 persons; all beautifully decorated and furnished. Suite of Rooms for family, well furnished and decorated. Dinners from 40 upwards 12 hours' notice. Cuisine first-class. Ices, Strawberries, Fruit and Cream in season. Coffees a speciality. Wines, Spirits, etc.; only best quality kept.—Proprietor, Arthur Mann (Manager with Carrick's Cafés and Restaurants for 25 years).

HILLCREST HOTEL, standing in its own grounds. First-class accommodation. Highly recommended. Billiards. Garage. Dinner (Table d'Hote) 7-30 p.m. Cuisine excellent and liberal. Separate tables. R.A.C. and A.A. appointments. Telegrams: Hillcrest.—T. MacMath, Proprietor.

Advert, *Alston Handbook*, 1924

This postcard, hand-dated June 1911, shows an army medical unit, commanded by Dr Harding? on the white horse. It was sent to Richard Welford, who had just purchased the Hillcrest. The men, who are possibly volunteers, are wearing khaki uniforms and red cross badges (not armbands), indicating a qualification. They are accompanied by eleven buglers and four snare drummers, with two ambulances taking up the rear. Those present took part in one-day manoeuvres on Middle Fell.

Alston Brewery, on the right, was built by Christopher Blackett & Co. in the 1770s. Over the years it was greatly extended, with the addition of a house, land, stables and cottages. It continued to be operated by them until its sale in 1845, when it was bought by Shaw, Gill & Co. (later John Gill & Co.). The purchase included three local inns – the Greyhound, Royal Oak and Dun Cow. Farmer John Gill (b.1809, Knaresdale) and his brother Railton (b.1811) were operating partners. Railton, a doctor and surgeon, lived at Brewery House from c.1851. He continued the business (Railton Gill & Co.) after John's death in the 1850s. John's sons, John Jr. (b.1845) and George (b.1848), who were shareholders and brewers, bought out the brewery and three inns in 1870 for £4,200. Railton moved to Dale View House where he died in 1882, aged 71. Having also acquired the Blue Bell, the 'new' John Gill & Co. collapsed in the late 1880s, leaving a Carlisle & Cumberland Bank debt of £4,287. The company's failure was attributed to a declining population and falling business and property values, factors which were noted as 'special circumstances which now attended business in Alston and neighbourhood'. John became a 'brewery traveller' in Newcastle, but widowed George, whose declining health was exacerbated by drink,

died at Alston in 1892 aged 44. His wife 'Minnie' (née Grieveson) was a Gateshead publican's daughter who had died in 1881, aged 28.

In 1894 the brewery site was purchased for £1,000 by George William Storey (b.1855, Alston), son of Thirlwall, druggist and dentist in the Potato Market. George was originally a draper, but by 1881 had become a woollen 'stocking & hose manufacturer' (items that were popular with women and miners at the time). Based at the old 'knitting shed' adjoining the woollen mill, he later employed up to 100 workers. His replacement 'Knit Hosiery Works' was converted from part of the old brewery and continued to operate until after his death in May 1940, aged 85 (although he had retired in about 1924).

After being a 'butter factory' (Alston Dairy Co.) for several years, the other brewery buildings and land were leased to Miss Mary M. Barton in 1902 to house 'Alston Laundry & Public Baths' (note the washing lines in the photograph). The business was continued by Miss Barton's associate, Elizabeth Blackett-Ord (d.1952, aged 90), until 1949 when it was transferred to the Carlisle Laundry Co. Both ladies lived at nearby Old Brownside (original farmhouse dated 1678), which was bought and rebuilt by Miss Blackett-Ord in 1901.

George W. Storey moved from West View to live in South Tyne (originally Brewery) House, letting out the four cottages that adjoined the works. He was described as one of 'Alston's most prominent residents' and an active businessman with 'long service in local government'. A member and later chairman of the Rural District Council (1897–1925), he was also a JP for 33 years from 1907, and chairman of the governors of Samuel King's School. In addition, he held other offices 'too numerous to mention'.

Above: billhead, 1859

Below: billhead and label, *c.*1847

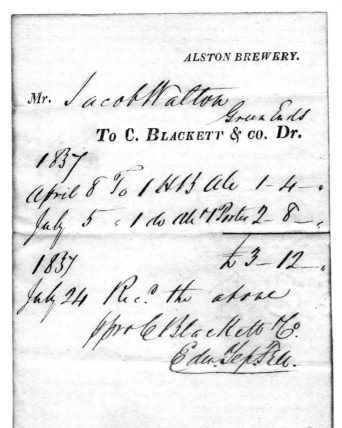

TO be SOLD, by AUCTION, at the House of Mrs. BLAND, the CROWN INN, ALSTON, Cumberland, on FRIDAY, the 28th of FEBRUARY, 1845, at Six o'Clock in the Evening, all that old-established and well-known COMMON BREWERY, situate at ALSTON, with the excellent Messuage or Dwelling-House, Garden, Meadow Field, Pasture, Cottages, Malting Houses, Stables, and Buildings adjoining thereto; and the Plant, Vats, and Casks, and all other Utensils and Materials belonging to the said Brewery. The Stock in Trade to be taken by the Purchaser at a Valuation.

Also all those THREE excellent and well-accustomed INNS or PUBLIC HOUSES, situate at ALSTON, called by the names of the ROYAL OAK, the GREYHOUND, and the DUN COW.

Above: invoice to Jacob Walton, Greenends, 1837
Right: advert, *Carlisle Journal,* for sale of Alston Brewery and three inns, 1 February 1845

Established in 1902, Alston Laundry first used horse-drawn transport, then Ford model Ts. This Willeys-Overland Crossley truck with canvas back, seen outside the laundry in 1926, was a later acquisition. Following a 1919 agreement between Crossley and W-O of the USA (mainly for cars, but also some commercials), chassis kits were shipped from Canada, then assembled and fitted with British bodies at Stockport, Manchester. Originally running on solid tyres, the front wheels of this vehicle have been replaced with pneumatics. The employee on the left is William Harold Coulthard (b.1889?, Garrigill), who by 1934 was registrar of births, marriages and deaths at the Town Hall. In the middle is Edward Bain (Bayne), who may have had family in Alston up to the 1880s. On the right is Mark Douglas, who was born at Tanfield, Durham, in 1893, and whose father was briefly (c.1901) landlord of the Blue Bell Inn. Mark worked for Miss Blackett-Ord from c.1907 to about 1949, later serving as a rural postman. He completed a round of twelve miles per day for thirteen years before retiring in 1966, aged 73 (d.1976).

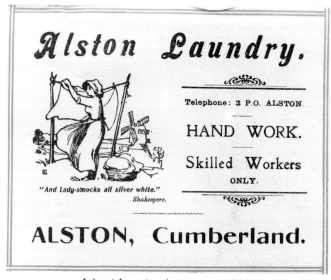

Advert from touring map, c.1920s

ALSTON LAUNDRY
AND PUBLIC BATHS.
NO CHEMICALS   Goods Collected
or Machinery used.   and Delivered.
Price Lists on application.

Advert, 1912

Lying close to the Tyne Bridge, the old corn mill seen here *c.*1890 formed part of Bridge End farm estate. This was bordered on the west by the original Penrith/Hartside road, which ran through Leadgate prior to the construction of the 1824 MacAdam Alston Turnpike Trust route. In 1697 there was a Quarter Session petition for £12–£14 for repairs to the old bridge over the river here. John Kirton, mason, had already been paid £4/10s for temporary work, and it was noted that 'if it should fall, £200 will not rebuild the same'. Renewed in 1757/8, the bridge was swept away, along with most others on the Tyne, in the 'Great Flood' of November 1771. In 1784 it was replaced by a 'high stone bridge of one arch', comprising a 66 foot span, with 12 feet between parapets and a drop of *c.*20 feet to the river bed. This cost £199/10s.

In 1833, with new roads completed, the old structure was deemed 'narrow and inconvenient'. The justices ordered a replacement bridge to be built costing a maximum of £1,400. Work on the single-span crossing began in July, but it was partly destroyed in an autumn flood. The old bridge alongside was temporarily repaired and builders Nixson & Denton of Carlisle were paid £74/8/9 to retrieve materials from the river. Having been redesigned with a double arch and re-tendered in 1835, the bridge was finally completed in its current form in June 1836 at a cost of *c.*£1,000. The brewery approach junction was also realigned away from the property.

Bridge End Mill was built *c.*1752 by Hewatson, the brother of the lead mine agent for Allgood, Loraine & Co, whose workmen were obliged to use it. It had a powerful undershot water wheel with a race fed from a dam on the river 350 feet upstream. When let to Henry Hutchinson in 1821 it included a drying kiln, barley mill and dwelling. By 1829 it was being run by miller Timothy Welsh (b.1799, Allendale), who also farmed the adjoining 60 acres, later assisted by his son William (b.1831).

This section of the river is known as 'The Doucker', and although the origins of the name are long forgotten, a *c.*1840s newspaper cutting describes the Sunday 'duckings' (baptisms) in Welsh's mill dam of about forty white-robed Mormon converts. Mr Russell had returned from America as a Mormon missionary, and hundreds lined the Firs walk opposite (on the left in this picture) to witness the spectacle of the baptisms. The Welshs left the mill after wife Jane's death in 1861 (aged 58) and it closed, business having diminished as a result of cheaper bulk produce carried in by rail. Timothy retired to daughter Mary's shop and house in the Market Place, where he died in 1885, aged 87, and son William became a colliery 'rolly [tramway] man' at Stockton. Mary (born *c.*1828) was a milliner and draper who first worked for Ann Pattinson, then ran her own business (opposite the Midland Bank) from the 1850s until *c.*1911.

Advert, *Carlisle Journal*, 20 April 1833

Many of the 'riflers' (as opposed to 'shooters', who hunted game) seen in this rare *c.*1886 Thomas Bramwell photograph were also members of Alston Volunteer Corps. The view looks down Black Burn from the bottom 'butt' of the 800 yard 'Rodderup' Rifle Range, which was adjacent to Rotherhope Fell Lead Mine, part owned and managed by corps member T.W. Crawhall Wilson. The group, complete with telescope and marker flag, are using Volunteer issue .455 calibre Martini-Henry rifles. The riflers included local 'notables' such as the Dickinsons (solicitor/bankers), Revd Edward Bowman (Vicar, RN), Samuel Kilburn (High School master), several Waltons (stationmaster, mine agents, farmer), Dr Stewart Carson and Drill Sergeant Reid.

The seventeenth century Blackburn Mill (corn), owned by Thomas Hudless in the 1690s, lies beyond the trees at Leadgate. Enlarged *c.*1768, it was operated by John Bell in the 1820s and George Thompson in the 1830s. He was followed by Joseph Pearson in the 1840s/50s and it was later tenanted by William Thompson. When advertised for sale in 1862 by owner John Irving of Plumpton, the mill comprised two pairs of stones, a barley mill, two drying kilns, a house and a 'never failing supply of water'. It seems to have closed down shortly after this time.

RIFLE MATCH AT ALSTON.

The return match between the 7th Northumberland (Allendale) and the 6th Cumberland (Alston) Rifle Volunteer Corps, each company being represented by eight of their crack shots, took place at the Rodderup Fell Range, near Alston, on Saturday last, when the former again scored a victory, but on this occasion by only seven points. The morning was wet and gloomy, but a fine afternoon was experienced, and the breeze being slight and the light good, the shooting, as will be observed below, was quite above the average standard. The distances were 200, 500, and 600 yards, seven shots at each range, any position; Wimbledon targets. The vic-

Report, *Alston Herald*, 3 August 1878

The same rifle group seen at Rotherhope Fell Mine. Both views include the prominent bearded figure (possibly Joseph Dickinson Sr.), and a white-hatted gent with a notebook, who may have been a scorer.

Rotherhope mines were first worked in the mid-1700s, and from 1827–80 were leased by the influential Wilson (later Crawhall) family. Afterwards they were taken over by the Rotherhope Fell Mining Co., which worked them until 1898. They then passed to the Belgian Vieille Montagne Co., which continued to operate until 1948 when mining ceased.

During much of the eighteenth and nineteenth centuries, the lead industry supported the bulk of the population on Alston Moor. The area was one of Britain's most important lead mining districts, and over 100 mines were usually in operation. Between 1737 and 1887 Alston Moor produced about two million bings (1 bing = 8 cwt.) of ore, with an estimated value of £7.7 million. By the 1880s the industry was in terminal decline, leading to increased hardship and migration, the effects cushioned slightly by rising zinc and fluorspar production. Many of those who remained relied on livestock farming for a livelihood. The old industrial landscape, with hundreds of derelict mine sites, is now promoted for heritage and tourism.

Seen on the right is the main entrance to Rotherhope Fell Mine, the stone-arched Blackburn (Low) Horse Level (there were 'Middle' and 'High' levels above). This bears the datestone 1838 and was driven 4,200 feet south, cutting first the Victoria then the Rotherhope Fell Vein. There, two shafts in stone-vaulted engine rooms (later containing hydraulic machinery) were sunk to workings below. Between 1827 and 1938 about 60,000 tons of lead concentrates were produced, with an additional c.14,000 tons of fluorspar between 1908 and 1948.

Blackburn (Low) Horse Level (photo Hugh Walton c.1910)

This traditional Alston winter view dates from 17 March 1947. It was taken outside the Turk's Head Inn by builder Tom Kearton. Such scenes led to familiar annual news reports of 'Hartside blocked', 'Alston cut off' and 'Town isolated', accompanied by descriptions of snow cutting teams and sledge transport. Despite 'climate change' and a succession of mild winters, similar media headlines can still appear at the first sign of snow. According to the *Hexham Courant* of February 1947, the old village 'sages' agreed that it was the 'worst ever winter for some 60 years', but maintained that conditions had been more severe in their youth, and that 'the wintry season is slowly becoming less robust'. Climatic data for Alston Moor up to *c.*1960 shows snow recorded in every month except July. The annual average snow covering at Alston was 40 days per year, with 55 days at Nenthead and 120 on Cross Fell summit (where it lay for 191 days in 1950/51). The lowest local temperature, -9°F (-23°C), was recorded at Nenthead in 1881.

Although opinions and records differ greatly, noted bad winters were regular occurrences. In February 1854 Christopher Oliver, aged 18, died on Killhope where his body lay for three weeks. 1874/75 was characterised by 'raging storms' and temperatures of 2°F (-17°C). In 1880/81 'early winter' storms began on 30 October with 15 inches of snow. Alston Skating Club was formed in December, the 'ice rink' created by flooding the Golden Lion field. The 'Black Tuesday' blizzards in January saw 17 feet of snow in places, along with severe frosts. The winter of 1895 began on 22 December 1894 with ten weeks of snowstorms, gales and intense frosts; Hartside was blocked for seven weeks. In 1901 the water in Ashgill waterfall froze solid, while *c.*1908 roads were impassable and an Italian miner's body was brought through the mines from Carrshield to Nenthead for burial. March 1916 was described as 'one continuous blizzard', the 'worst storm for 21 years', and in the following year from January to March there was a 'series of severe snowstorms'. 1940 and 1941 saw long and persistent heavy snowfalls, with 'enormous drifts' – during one storm in February 1941 it 'snowed for over 50 hours'. The 'wash-out' summer of 1946 was followed by the 'worst winter in living memory' in 1947. During the seven weeks of frost, snow and blizzards, RAF Dakotas dropped hay and feed to isolated farms, and to compound the misery there were severe rainstorms and floods in April. 1963 was described as 'one of the worst winters on record', beginning in December 1962 and continuing until March. There were reports of 'snow piled up to roof height' (one farmer had a cow on the roof!) and 'great intensity of frost'. RAF helicopters dropped feed, and again there was flooding in April and May. 1985/86 was probably the last 'bad' winter, with many later southern 'immigrants' believing the past weather anecdotes to be nothing more than discouraging propaganda!

EARLY ALSTON PHOTOGRAPHERS

As the business and commercial centre of the important Alston Moor lead mining area (approximately 58 square miles), Alston was a busy, bustling place during the later eighteenth and nineteenth centuries. The hard working, resourceful and independent nature of its inhabitants is reflected in the many old photographs that survive, some dating back to the 1860s.

The first professional photographer, **Richard Von Dix**, was a remarkable and enigmatic figure who appeared in about 1868. It is not known why he took up residence in such a remote district, but he left behind an outstanding and diverse pictorial legacy. His work displays a broad technical ability, ranging from single portraits and groups taken in both indoor studio and outdoor booth, to town scenes and landscapes.

Richard (b.1834) was the youngest of three sons (Thomas b.1831, William b.1832). He was born at Llanrhidian, Glamorgan to John Dix and Mary Owens (from nearby Oxwich parish) who married at Llanrhidian Church on 29 May 1829. John, a corn miller at the Low Mill, died in 1835 aged 43. When his wife died in 1838 aged 38, the orphaned siblings were left as parish paupers. After absconding from his employer and guardian, Richard was later described by the magistrate as 'quite a lad'. Thomas remained a weaver in Llanrhidian, while his brothers Richard (1861, artist photographer with 'Tucker's Portrait Van') and William are listed separately as photographers in North Yorkshire in the early 1860s. They later formed the South Wales Photographic Co. at Eastborough (Scarborough), adding 'Von' to their names. After a dispute, William moved to Grimsby ('Royal Dock Photographic Salon') where he died in 1889. Richard relocated to Alston, where he was also noted as a conjuror, vocalist and dramatic performer! His early works include photographs of the original Kirkhaugh Church, rebuilt in 1868, several of Alston old church (demolished in 1869) and views of Nent Hall, the Market Cross and the Walton Memorial dated 1870. Outdoor scenes

were then less appealing to many photographers because the glass negatives produced by the messy wet collodion process needed immediate darkroom facilities. This necessitated the use of a portable studio. Most of the images he produced were of standard 'carte de visite' size (4 x 2½ inches) mounted on card.

Whilst photographers proliferated in urban areas during the 1870s, few of them established studios in rural districts. Instead, these usually had to rely on occasional visits by itinerant operators, some of dubious character. In 1871 Von Dix was resident in Edmunds (later Grisdale's) Lane, operating on a seasonal basis, but by 1874 he was advertising an 'all year round all weather service' at his 'splendid Crystal Studio' at Townfoot. Short exposure times were dependant on good light, so weather and season had a critical effect on indoor photography. As a result, many of his portrait shots show steadying devices to keep the subjects still – chairs, pedestal stands and hidden neck braces were commonly used. Early outdoor group pictures, including several of nearby Leadgate schoolchildren (why two boys with twenty-nine girls?) and those taken in his tent studio (with occasional glimpses of grass!) relied on bright conditions. The classic view of four lead miners, illustrated here, has the bonus of their names written on the reverse: Thomas Walton, James Spottiswood, John Teasdale and Robert Walton.

In February 1877 Von Dix moved to the Sportsman's Arms (half a mile south-west of Alston), although he continued to visit adjoining districts and local fairs with his portable studio. Later in the decade the printed photo backs gave way to a handwritten type, usually including the name Smedley, suggesting an assistant or partner. These backs were subsequently replaced by two fancy 'Excelsior' versions, carrying both their names. Records show the new associate to be Georgina Smedley (b.1851, Lincoln, the eldest of ten siblings), who is noted as both a 'photo artist' and 'photographer'. By 1881 they had left Alston, appearing in Jarrow as a married couple. Sometime later they set up a photographic business at Mount Pleasant in Consett where Richard died in August 1888, aged 54. He was buried at Blackhill Cemetery. Georgina later worked for a photographer in Rochdale, eventually returning to Lincoln where she died and was buried in March 1903. In 1881, three of her sisters, one in Lincoln and two in Newcastle, were recorded as 'photo artists'.

Thomas Bramwell (b.1835, Garrigill) opened a watchmaker and jeweller's shop in Front Street c.1860. There is no evidence of his involvement in photography before Von Dix left the district. Early Bramwell pictures date from about 1884, and he dominated the local market for the next twenty years. Greatly improved dry gelatine plates, which could be prepared and used at leisure, were in use by then and gave photographers a new freedom. In addition to portrait work, for which he opened a new studio at the rear of his

VON DIX. ALSTON.
PHOTO ARTIST. CUMBERLAND.

premises in the early 1890s, Thomas took large numbers of local town and landscape views, selling these in his shop. After 1900 many were produced in postcard form, both by himself and at a later period by numerous other companies.

Kirkhaugh Church

Thomas died in February 1907 and the photographic side of the business declined under his son Charles, who ran the shop until his death in 1925.

Hugh Walton (b.1859, Alston), a tinsmith, spent most of his life as an ironmonger. The family's first shop opened in

Leadgate schoolchildren

Front Street *c.*1880, just above Bramwell's, later crossing the road to the Potato Market where it remained until after his death in 1928, aged 69.

Hugh took up photography later in life, specialising in outdoor and landscape work. From about 1900 his output increased and filled much of the gap left by Thomas Bramwell's retirement and death. Many of his photos – which often carry the initials HWA (Hugh Walton Alston) – were displayed and sold at his shop. The 'people's photographer', he recorded a wide variety of local events and scenes, sometimes working in difficult situations and inclement conditions. He encouraged others, his premises later including a 'Dark Room for Hire'. Hugh Walton liked to title his work, but never quite mastered the art of writing (and spelling) on the negatives in reverse. Another competent photographer who operated at this period and signed his work JLD (Dickinson?) also suffered the same affliction.

In addition to these notable artists, many other photographers appeared during the post-1900 picture postcard boom years. They include T.W. Tatters of Alston, Gibson of Hexham, Johnston of Gateshead (Monarch Series) and a multitude of publishers who used the work of others. Unfortunately, many stood in the same place to take their photographs of the town, resulting in a large number of repetitious views, some of which were in production for several decades.

Advert, 17 October 1874, *Alston Herald*

Advert, 18 April 1874, *Alston Herald*

Above: Thomas Bramwell photo mount back
Right: Dix & Smedley 'Carte de Visite' decorated photograph mount back

ALSTON MOOR POPULATION

Year	Total population	Variation	Alston township (where available) excl. workhouse	Houses in Alston: inhabited (I) & uninhabited (U)
1774	c.3,900*			*(est. by Wallace, 1890)
1801	4,746			
1811	5,079	+333		
1821	5,699	+620	1,870	
1831	6,858	+1,159		
1841	6,062	-796	1,650	382 I & 38 U = 420
1851	6,816*	+754	2005	413 I & 4 U = 417 *(Figures include 106 labourers and their families employed on railway works)
1861	6,404	-412	1,700	396 I & 49 U = 445
1871	5,680	-724	1,516	355 I & 56 U = 441
1881	4,621	-1,059	1,360	330 I & 48 U = 378
1891	3,384	-1,237	1,050	279 I & 94 U = 373
1901	3,134	-250	916	256 I & 41 U = 297
1911	3,075	-59		
1921	3,344	+269		
1931	2,678	-666		
1939*	2,889	+211		*(National Civilian Register)
1951	2,327	-562		
1961	2,105	-222		
1971	1,916	-189		
1981	1,968	+52		
1991	2,057	+89		
2001	2,156	+99		

NOTES

- the census registration area covered 35,060 acres prior to 1861 and 36,971 thereafter.
- lead mining developments led to remote Alston Moor being a relatively densely populated rural area during the later eighteenth and much of the nineteenth centuries, with numbers peaking in 1831 and 1851. The onset of the industry's collapse in the late 1860s resulted in a rapid depopulation over the next three decades (a 45 per cent drop from 1871 to 1901). This had a marked effect on local trade and services.
- separate Alston town figures for 1861–1901 show a 46 per cent reduction in residents, with the number of inhabited houses across the region falling from 1,282 to 773 (about a 40 per cent drop) during the same period, lowering both property prices and rents.
- the current (2001) population is about one third of that of 150 years ago (1851).

BIBLIOGRAPHY

Alston with Garrigill and Nenthead, Parish Handbooks 1923-1928 et al

Alston Moor Paine Roll & Drift Roll (1597), typescript copies, 1908

Allan J.W., *North Country Sketches*, Newcastle Courant, 1881

Bell Dr T.M., Transport Development in the South Tyne Valley, notes for South Tynedale Railway *c*.2001

Burgess J., *A History of Cumbrian Methodism*, Titus Wilson, 1980

Caine Revd Caesar, *Cappella de Gerardgile*, R.M. Saint (Printer), 1908

Clues J.A., *History of Alston Parish Church from 1154*, typescript copy (*c*.1940)

Crick W.F. & Wadsworth J.E., *A Hundred Years of Joint Stock Banking*, Hodder & Stoughton (1936, 4th Ed. 1964)

Hicks W.B., *A History of the Parish Church of St Augustine, Alston*, 1955 (Revised 1996)

Hood K., *The Co-operative Societies of the North Pennines*, North Pennines Heritage Trust, 2001

Hoole K., *North Eastern Branch Line Termini*, Oxford Publishing, 1985

Hopton Revd H.C., *Congregationalism in the Parish of Alston*, W. Etchells, 1904

Hunter T., *The Alston Foundry Story, World War II*, typescript copy (*c*.1992)

Jenkins S.C., *The Alston Branch*, Oakwood Press, 1991

MacBride M., *Quaint Alston*, Herald Printing Co., no date (*c*.1920)

Nall Revd W., *A Hand Book to Alston*, Wordsworth Press, 1888

Page I.E., *Walks Around Alston*, Editions 1-5 (1893-1912), W. Etchells

Patterson W.M., *Northern Primitive Methodism*, E. Dalton, 1909

Penfold Dr J.B., *The Clock Makers of Cumberland*, Brampton Historical Society, 1976

Pennypacker C.H., 'A Trip to England', *The Mineral Collector* Vol 11, 1904; also Vol 2, 1895

Robertson A., *A History of Alston Moor*, Bookcase, 1998

Robertson A., *Articles in Alston Moor Newsletter*, 1996-2004

Sopwith T., 'An Account of the Mining Districts of Alston Moor, Weardale and Teesdale', W. Davison, 1833. (Davis Books 1984)

Vale E., *North Country*, Batsford, 1937

Wainwright A., *A Pennine Journey*, Penguin Books, 1987

Wallace W., *Alston Moor: Its Pastoral People: Its Mines and Miners*, Mawson, Swan & Morgan, 1890

Wilkinson P., *The Nent Force Level and Brewery Shaft*, North Pennines Heritage Trust, 2001

Information was also extracted from the following:

County histories, trade directories and gazetteers (1774-1940)

Records of the Greenwich Hospital Estates, London Lead Company, Alston with Garrigill Rural District Council and Parish Council, Quarter Sessions and Alston Petty Sessions

Alston Moor Manorial Records

Parish and civil registers

Census returns and summaries (1801-2001)

CWAA Society transactions

Notes, diaries, etc. of: Tom Kearton, Revd W. Nall, Joseph Pearson, John Walton Robinson, W.H. Thompson, William Thompson, William Wallace, Revd N.A. Walton et al

Newspapers: *Alston Herald & East Cumberland Advertiser, Carlisle Journal, Carlisle Patriot, Cumberland & Westmorland Herald, Hexham Courant, Newcastle Journal & Evening Chronicle*

Maps: OS 25" (1:2500) Cumberland sheets 33, 34, 41, 42 (1859) First edition and revised (1898) Second edition; OS 6" (1:10560) sheets NY64&74 published 1957

The author's collection of documents, illustrations, maps, photographs, postcards, books and ephemera

ABBREVIATIONS

Greenwich Hospital. Royal Hospital for Seamen at Greenwich in Kent, formed in 1692, now administered by the Admiralty Board. Alston Moor formed part of their large 'Northern Estates' between 1735 and 1964 (229 years in control)

RDC. Rural District Council, referring to 'Alston with Garrigill Rural District Council', formed in 1894, ceased 1974 (80 years in control)

CCC. Cumberland [now Cumbria] County Council

SKS. Samuel King's School, built in 1909, moved to new site in 1957

London Lead Company (LLCo. or Gov. & Co.). Officially 'The Governor & Company for the Smelting down of Lead with Pittcoale and Seacoale', granted royal Charter in 1692, informally sometimes referred to as 'The Quaker Co.' They were the largest lead mining/smelting company on Alston Moor from 1745; left the district in 1882. (Active in the area since 1705.)